CW00404232

Birmingham Repertory Theatre Company
presents

Twins

By Maureen Lawrence

First Performance at
The Door, Birmingham Repertory Theatre
on 7 October 1998

SUPPORTED BY
THE NATIONAL LOTTERY
THROUGH
THE **ARTS COUNCIL**
OF ENGLAND

Providing Theatre for Birmingham

Confidence

by Judy Upton

Wed 23 Sep - Wed 25 Nov

'...So what do you want to be? The kicker or the kicked?'

Join the schemers and dreamers on the seafront, as another summer season begins and there's serious money to be made. Amongst the paint-peeling kiosks on the prom, Ella arrives like an erotic whirlwind, hellbent on securing the elusive jackpot. But everyone else is raising their game too and, as events race towards an explosive conclusion, a pet hamster lies frozen amongst the melting Mivvis.

Award-winning playwright Judy Upton's many prizes include the George Devine Award in 1993, two Guinness Awards and most recently the Open Stages Competition in 1997 which she won with her play *To Blusher With Love*.
Director: Anthony Clark
Designer: Patrick Connellan
Lighting: Tim Mitchell

After Dark: Tue 24 Nov (post show)

Twins

by Maureen Lawrence

Wed 7 Oct - Wed 18 Nov

'We're like a pantomime horse with two front ends. We don't fit the bill.'

Perched in the attic cluttered with their last few remaining heirlooms, Mimi and Gigi await the imminent arrival of the men who will repossess their home. But, Gigi believes, their hopelessly tangled lives, a husband tasted by them both and her last, mad spending spree mean that they are going to have to finally face facts. Elegant and sharply funny , Twins explores a relationship that runs through three very different solutions to the one problem.

Maureen Lawrence's previous work has been performed at both the Derby Playhouse and West Yorkshire Playhouse and her play *Resurrection* was the winner of the LWT Plays on Stage Award.
Director: Simon Usher
Designer: Lucy Weller
Lighting: Tim Mitchell

After Dark: Tue 17 Nov (post show)

Down Red Lane

by Kate Dean

Wed 28 Oct - Sat 28 Nov

'We've made it. We've f**kin' made it. Two thousand f**kin' years n' we made it'

It is Christmas 1999, not that you'll see any tinsel in the Red Lane Quarry - a time of reflection, fear and the odd splutter of hope. Through the dense winter fog, Spider and his ragbag of mates emerge, killing time with anything from a battered old saxophone to a bag of glue. Beneath them, the city pulses with distant light and movement - as it prepares for the celebration of the century.

Winner of a Special Prize in the Mobil Playwriting competition, *Down Red Lane* is just one of many award-winning plays by Kate Dean. Her play Rough (winner of the John Whiting Award) was produced in the Birmingham Rep Studio in 1994.
Director: Anthony Clark
Designer: Patrick Connellan
Lighting: Tim Mitchell

After Dark: Tue 10 Nov (post show

Sep 98 - Jan 99

Birmingham's only venue dedicated to new writing

Tickets: £9.00
Concs: £7.00
Standby: £5.00 (from
1pm on day of
performance)

Sounds In Session

by Tyrone Huggins and The Theatre of Darkness

Thu 10 Dec - Sat 12 Dec

Theatre for the twenty-first century

Tanya's been on TOTP. Twice! She's also heard Black Voices. She wanted to do what Prince did. Turn her back on the whole bloody lot! She almost did what Jacko did. Turned her self white!
She has to prove at least one thing. She is in control.

Set in a grubby basement recording studio, three people gather to record one track that will change their lives. But which track? Written as a twelvetrack album Sounds...In Session pollutes your ear with what really controls the music biz...the technology !
Director: Tyrone Huggins
Design: Kendra Ullyart

Fourteen Songs, Two Weddings And A Funeral

Tamasha Theatre Company and Birmingham Repertory Theatre Company

Tue 15 Dec - Sat 9 Jan

The blockbuster Bollywood movie comes to the stage with a new English adaptation. Tear jerking melodrama, song, dance, comedy, tragedy, glamour, romance, lavish sets and sparkling costumes. Birmingham Rep and Tamasha Theatre Company have co-produced four new plays over the past five years - *Shaft of Sunlight*, *A Yearning*, *Tainted Dawn* and the multi- award winning *East is East* by Ayub Khan-Din.

Adapted from the film *Hum Aapke Hain Koun* for the stage by Sudha Bhuchar and Kristine Landon-Smith.
Director and Choreographer: Kristine Landon-Smith
Set Design: Sue Mayes
Lighting Design: Paul Taylor
Musical Director: Colin Sell

After Dark: Tue 5 Dec (post show)

De Profundis

Moving Theatre

13 - 29 Jan

Written in Reading Gaol to Wilde's lover and nemesis Alfred Douglas, *De Profundis* is both and astonishing tour-de-force of self-analysis and a passionate cry for us to re-examine all our attitudes and assumptions about crime and punishment.

Edited by Merlin Holland
Performed by Corin Redgrave
Music Composed by Jonathan Goldstein
Each performance will be followed by a discussion on the issues raised.

Just, Not Fair

Moving Theatre

11 - 30 Jan

Jim Robinson, one of the Bridgewater Four who won their freedom in 1997 after a marathon campaign proving their innocence, has fashioned *Just, Not Fair* with director Jessica Dromgoole and actor Malcolm Tierney.

It is an extraordinary monologue about his life including 18 years spent in prison and his time on the outside.
Production Design: Phillippe Brandt
Lighting Design: Jim Simmons
Each performance will be followed by a discussion on the issues raised in the play.

Twins
By Maureen Lawrence

CAST

Mimi Amelda Brown

Gigi Anne White

Director Simon Usher

Designer Lucy Weller

Lighting Design Tim Mitchell

Assistant Director Phillip Tinline

Stage Manager Niki Ewen

Deputy Stage Manager Ruth Morgan

Assistant Stage Manager Daniel Precious

Maureen Lawrence
Author

Maureen Lawrence was born and educated in Leeds, read English at Nottingham University, taught for a while and then went to America, where she studied at Michigan University, and began writing, winning the prestigious Hopwood Award for new writing. Her first novel *The Tunnel* was published in both Britain and America; a second novel *Shadow On The Wall* followed two years later. A third book *A Telling And A Keeping* was published by The Women's Press in 1990. The long gap between books was filled by raising a family, teaching, writing, and latterly, learning to be a playwright.

Commissioned by Annie Castledine to write two plays for Northern Studio Theatre - *Tokens Of Affection* and *Black Ice*, she became a theatre writer almost by accident. Her plays include the highly acclaimed *Father's Day*, commissioned by West Yorkshire Playhouse; *Resurrection* which won the LWT Plays on Stage Award for Paines' Plough; and *Real Writing* commissioned by Moving Theatre at Riverside.

She has also devised and written many plays for young people with T.I.E companies and students; and has written a translation of *Antigone* for Communicado Theatre Company. Maureen Lawrence sees herself as a belated convert to theatre, finding in drama a form of communication more direct and sometimes more satisfying than prose. She likes asking awkward questions. In *Twins*, commissioned for Birmingham Rep's season of new plays, she tried hard to come up with answers and ended by going round in circles. She is currently working on projects for film, radio, another play for West Yorkshire Playhouse and a new book.

Amelda Brown
(Mimi)

Trained: Royal Academy of Dramatic Art

Theatre: *Like a Dancer* (New End Theatre); *Importance Of Being Earnest* (Colchester); *Chaste Maid in Cheapside* (The Globe); *Wishbones, Waiting At The Water's Edge* (Bush Theatre); *Light Shining In Buckinghamshire* (National Theatre); *Beautiful Thing* (Duke of York/Donmar); *The Swan* (Traverse); *When We Are Married* (West Yorkshire Playhouse); *Kafka's Dick* (Birmingham Rep); *Just Between Ourselves* (Old Vic); *Miss Julie* (Oldham); *Our Country's Good* (Leicester); *The Relapse, Village Wooing, The Lover, A Midsummer Night's Dream, The Real Thing* (Birmingham Rep); *My Heart's A Suitcase* (Royal Court); *Apart From George* (National Theatre & Royal Court); *Fire In The Lake, Power Of The Dog* (Joint Stock); *Trafford Tanzi, Cider With Rosie* (Bolton); *Falkland Sound* (Coventry); *Top Girls* (Leicester).

Television. Her many television appearances include: *Playing The Field, Trial by Jury, The Bill, Thin Blue Line, Pie In The Sky, Grange Hill, Back Up, Ellington, Class Act, Soldier Soldier, Sibling Rivalry, Mayhew's London, Minder, Chandler And Co, A Touch Of Frost, The Bill, Lovejoy, Casualty, Peak Practice, Medics, Seconds Out, Shrinks, Capital City, The Rainbow, The Practice* and *Sherlock Holmes.*

Film: *Candle In The Dark* (Lantern Film); *My Sister In This House* (World Film); *Dakota Road* (Working Title); *Spirit* (Elephant Rock); *Hope And Glory*

(Davros); *Little Dorrit* (Sands); *An English Christmas* (Film On Four); *Biddy* (Sands).

Radio: *Parklife, Up And Running, Mr Clean, Kiss Me Quick, The Fool, The People's Woman* (BBC).

Anne White
(Gigi)

Trained: Webber Douglas Academy

Theatre: *The Weavers* (Gate Theatre); *Voyage In The Dark* (Sphinx Theatre Co, Young Vic & tour); *Richard III* (English Shakespeare Co); *Sir Thomas More* (Shaw Theatre); *Mrs Gaskell & Miss Bronte* (Harrogate Theatre); *Don't Fool With Love* (Cheek By Jowl); *Abigail's Party* (Cambridge Theatre Co); *My Father's House* (Birmingham Rep); *The Voysey Inheritance* (Royal Lyceum); *The Stronger, The Unknown General, The Late, See The Pretty Lights*, (Actor's Studio Theatre); *Night Must Fall, Towards Zero* (Connaught, Worthing); *Taming of The Shrew* (Spectrum Theatre); *Roots, The Devil's Disciple, The Royal Pardon* (Orchard Theatre); *Twelfth Night* (Stage 77); *Arms and the Man, The Miser, Liberty Hall* (Pitlochry Theatre); *Something Borrowed* (Gate Theatre); *Othello* (Theatre Space); *Vanity Fair, Andromache, Midsummer Night's Dream, The Man Of Mode, Twelfth Night, The Cid, Macbeth, A Family Affair* (Cheek By Jowl).

Television: *The Bill, General Hospital, Kids, God Speed, Shine On Harvey Moon.*

Film: *The Old Curiosity Shop* (Disney Productions), *State Of Wonder* (International Pictures).

Simon Usher
Director

Simon works regularly at the National Theatre Studio, developing new plays and researching classics, and has previously been Resident Director at Riverside Studios, Literary Manager at the Royal Court Theatre, Associate Director at Leicester Haymarket, and Joint Artistic Director at Belgrade Theatre Coventry.

Previous directing credits include: *Wishbones, All of You Mine, The Mortal Ash, Not Fade Away, Pond Life* (for which he won Best Director in the London Fringe Awards), *The Evil Doers*, (Bush Theatre); *The Wolves* (Paines Plough Tour and Bridewell Theatre); *Exquisite Sister, Burning Everest* (West Yorkshire Playhouse); *Whole Lotta Shakin ', Hamlet, Heartbreak House, The Browining Version, Waiting For Godot, Les Liaisons Dangeureuses* (Coventry Belgrade Theatre); *No Man's Land* (English Touring Theatre); *Trios, Sister Streams, Sand Play, The Trial* (Riverside Studios); *Three Judgments in One* (Gate Theatre); *King Baby* (RSC Pit); *Can't Stand Up for Falling Down* (Palace Theatre Watford); *Three Judgements in One* (Gate Theatre); *Lettice and Lovage, The Winters Tale, Trios, The Lovers Melancholy, The Naked, Pericles, Murders in The Rue Morgue, Pale Performer, Looking At You (Revived) Again; The Bells, The Broken Heart, French Without Tears, Timon of Athens, The War in Heaven,* (Leicester Haymarket and Royal Court); *Timon Of Athens* (National Theatre Studio), *True Love Romances, The Guest Room* (Old Red Lion); *Ladies in Waiting* (Finborough); *Swan Killer* (Snape Maltings); *Women Undressed and*

Bodies To Be Dispatched (Royal Lyceum, Edinburgh and Croydon Warehouse); *The Open Couple* (Croydon Warehouse).

Lucy Weller
Designer

Lucy Weller studied theatre design under Margaret Harris at Riverside Studios. She has designed for the Royal Court Theatre, The Traverse, Theatre de Complicite and the Royal National Theatre. She has designed many shows for Nancy Meckler including *Abingdon Square*, *Low Level Panic* and *A Street Car Named Desire*. Lucy recently returned to study illustration at the Royal College of Art where she won the Folio Prize. Since then she has designed a fashion show for Bella Freud, costumes for *My Fair Lady* at the Sheffield Crucible and costumes for Howard Barker's new play *Ursula*. She has recently designed the costumes for the Birmingham Rep's production of *Hamlet*.

Tim Mitchell
Lighting Designer

Tim is currently lighting designer in residence at Birmingham Repertory Theatre where he has lit many productions, these include: *Frozen*, *Whisper of Angels Wings*, *The Cherry Orchard*, *True Brit*, *Dr Jekyll and Mr Hyde*, *Romeo and Julie*, *The Merchant of Venice*, *Macbeth*, *Old Times*, *Peter Pan* and *The Atheist's Tragedy* (Gold Medal Winner at the 1995 Prague Quadrennial).

Other productions include: *Romeo and Juliet* (RSC), *The Red Balloon* and *The Alchemist* (Royal National Theatre), *Outside of Heaven, Inventing a New Colour* and *Young Writers Festival* (Royal Court Theatre), *Someone to Watch Over Me, When We are Married, Landslide, The Winslow Boy* and *The Entertainer* (West Yorkshire Playhouse) *Dead Funny, Wallflowering* and *Tess of the D'Urbervilles* (Salisbury Playhouse), *Song at Sunset* and the New Directions Season (Hampstead THeatre), *Adam Bede, A Passionate Woman, The Importance of Being Earnest, Les Liasons Dangereuses* and *Our Boys* (Derby Playhouse), *A Soldiers Song* (Theatre Royal Stratford East), *WodeHouse on Broadway* (BBC TV/Theatre Royal Plymouth), *As You Like It* and *Anthony and Cleopatra* (English Shakespeare Company).

Phil Tinline
Assistant Designer

As Assistant Director at the Orange Tree Theatre, Richmond: *What the Heart Feels*; *Family Circles*; *She'll be Coming Round The Mountain*; *Romeo & Juliet*; *The Outside*; *A Midsummer Night's Dream*.

Other directing credits include: *A Glass of Water*, *She'll Be Wearing Silk Pyjamas* (Orange Tree); *Shakespeare for Breakfast* (Edinburgh Fringe); *Lavender Song* (Prince Theatre); *Rum and Vodka, Newsrevue* (Canal Cafe Theatre).

Phil is at Birmingham Rep for a year under the Regional Theatre Young Director Scheme, before which he ran the Canal Cafe Theatre in West London.

The Birmingham Repertory Theatre Company
Introducing

The Door

Since it was founded in 1913 Birmingham Repertory Theatre Company has been a leading national company. Its programming has introduced a range of new and foreign plays to the British theatre repertoire, and it has been a springboard for many internationally famous actors, designers and directors.

As the arts in Birmingham have grown in stature, with the opening of Symphony Hall, the achievements of the City of Birmingham Symphony Orchestra and the arrival of the Birmingham Royal Ballet so there has been massive investment in the resident theatre company.

Now the company can present classic, new and discovery plays on a scale appropriate to one of the largest acting spaces in Europe , as well as a consistent programme of new theatre in its studio, by some of the brightest contemporary talent To celebrate this, the space has a new name and a new look.

The Door's programme seeks to find a young and culturally diverse audience for the theatre, through the production of new work in an intimate, flexible space - work, that reflects, defines and enhances their experience of the world while introducing them to the possibilities of the medium.

New Work at Birmingham Repertory Theatre
– past, present and future

In recent years, this theatre has produced a range of popular, award-winning and critically acclaimed new plays. These include *Divine Right* (1996), Peter Whelan's examination of the future of the British monarchy, Kate Dean's *Rough* (1994), Bryony Lavery's *Nothing Compares To You* (1995), Debbie Isitt's *Squealing Like A Pig* (1996), Ayub Khan-Din's *East is East* (1996) (co-production with Tamasha Theatre Company and the Royal Court Theatre, London), Ken Blakeson's *True Brit* (1997) and Nick Stafford's *The Whisper of Angel's Wings* (1997).

This year, our production of *Frozen* by Bryony Lavery which starred Anita Dobson, Tom Georgeson and Josie Lawrence was unaminously praised for its bravery, humanity and humour in exploring the intertwined experiences of a mother, the murderer of her daughter and the psychiatrist who treats him.

From this autumn the increased level of financial support for the theatre means that we can plan a range of creative projects and initiatives across the full range of theatre's spaces and activities, supporting both the artists who create new work and the audiences for it.

One example is **Transmissions** - a pilot project in which young people in Birmingham aged from 7 to 25 will write their own plays alongside experienced professional playwrights with the chance to see their work performed here at the theatre. Another is the theatre's attachment scheme for writers. This enables both younger and more experienced playwrights to explore new ideas and directions with our support and with the ultimate aim of transforming them into plays for our stages.

If you would like more information on this of other aspects of our work, please contact us on 0121 236 6771 x2108/2109

Ben Payne
Literary Manager

Frozen: Anita Dobson and Tom Georgeson
Photo: Robert Day

The Whisper of Angels' Wings: Tricia Kelly and Michael Cashman
Photo: Robert Day

The Birmingham Repertory Theatre gratefully acknowledges the support of the Sir Barry Jackson Trust in its new work development programme

THE SIR BARRY JACKSON TRUST

Birmingham Rep Young Writers Group

This autumn sees the relaunch of The Rep's Young Writers' Group. Building on its past successes the group will also be integrating the writers' work more closely with other new writing and production activities in The Door.

The young writers' group has an illustrious past. During 1996 - 98 the creative writing tutor was local writer Sarah Woods, whose plays *Grace, Nervous Women* and *Bidding and Binding* were performed at the Rep. For the past two years the Rep has also run a young writers' festival called Hot Off The Page.

Highlights of the work produced during the festival include *Redemption Denied* by Lucy Hughes, which took a hard hitting view of Birmingham drug culture, while *No Time to Say Goodbye* by Rachael Owen told the story of a young evacuee who rebels against his mother's religious fanaticism. Marie Clarke's *Apocalypse* took a satirical view of 90s female obsessions, careers, figures, boyfriends and food. In 1998 the youth theatre also performed Louise Ramsden's play *The Highwayman* - a black comedy about a disabled spinster who dreams of escape from the sister she is bound to care for

and the hidden secret that still overshadows their lives. Louise has workshopped other pieces with professional actors and in '96 her play *My Baby Mine* received a reading at the Royal Court Theatre Upstairs.

Many members of the Young Writers' Group have continued to develop their writing through higher education courses such as Theatre Arts or Drama at University.

Now the theatre is in a position to widen access to the group and to restructure the group's activities for regular tutorials by a resident tutor with visiting or guest tutors from the profession, in addition to specialised skills development workshops with other theatre practitioners such as directors and actors.

For more information about the Birmingham Rep Young Writers Group please call Liz Ingrams at The Rep on 0121 236 6771 x2109.

Transmissions

A festival of playwriting by young people

September to November 1998

As Birmingham's only venue dedicated to new writing The Door is investing in writers of the future, with an exclusive festival of playwriting for young people.

Something for all ages

Plays will be workshopped and developed with five primary schools, a Saturday playwriting project run for youth drama group members (drawn from Stage 2, Yeh-leh-leh Theatre Company, Kaos Theatre Company, SAMPAD, Swanshurst School and Streetwise Theatre Company), and a relaunched young writers group.

A chance to work alongside professionals

Everyone involved will work in collaboration with the Birmingham Rep's literature and education departments as well as their designated tutors. These professionals have been chosen for their ability to write, direct and work well with young people and include some of the region's most talented artists. Those taking part include local playwright and performer Lorna Laidlaw, Peter Wynne-Wilson, Maya Chowdhry (author of Birmingham Rep's most recent community production *Kaahini*), Glen Supple (a Royal Court Young People's Theatre director), Noel Grieg, Theresa Heskins and Sarah Woods.

Developing and performing new work

The project will have a different emphasis depending on the age range of the people involved. Children's groups will develop plays in conjunction with their teachers and tutors, other groups will develop and rehearse a series of linked scenes. Meanwhile young playwrights will work on a fifteen minute script and receive one to one tuition from playwright Sarah Woods with additional skills development workshops with other writers and practitioners. The best pieces will be directed by Theresa Heskins and rehearsed at the end of November, and others will receive rehearsed readings directed by an 'in-house' director over the two week period. The festival will culminate with performances at The Rep involving both professional and young actors.

For more information about this and any other Education activities please call Rachel Gartside, Head of Education on 0121 236 6771.

From Stage to Page

A stimulating programme of work for further and higher education groups to accompany the three new plays premiering in rep in The Door: **CONFIDENCE** by Judy Upton, **TWINS**, by Maureen Lawrence, and **DOWN RED LANE**, by Kate Dean.

What's On Offer?

Workshops

If you make block bookings, two workshops will be offered. The first involves an exploration of the content of the text, themes and structure etc. to be led by the Rep's Education Department and held at your college. The second will be run by a writer and the Rep's Associate Director Anthony Clark and will explore ideas behind the writing and the process of producing the piece from page to stage. These second workshops will take place at the theatre.

Scripts

Scripts will be produced for each play, and will provide an opportunity for further study of the text's form and content.

Discounted Tickets

Tickets are available at just £5.00 per performance. With tickets normally at £9/£7 this represents a substantial discount.

Unbeatable Value

Tickets, workshops and scripts are included in the price of the package. From Stage to Page is a pro-active approach to serve mutual needs – an opportunity to tackle your curriculum in a unique, accessible way, at the cutting edge of contemporary theatrical culture – all for just £25.00 per student (minimum 15 students).

After Darks

Held after the show with the company. Ask anything you've ever wanted to know about the play...an immediate, informal and inviting opportunity to question the play and the players - and it's free! After Darks in The Door will usually involve an expert panel who can debate the issues or concerns of the piece and set it in a wider context. Check the brochure or call our Box Office on 0121 236 4455 for dates.

Maureen Lawrence
Twins

faber and faber

First published in 1998
by Faber and Faber Limited
3 Queen Square London WC1N 3AU

Typeset by Country Setting, Woodchurch, Kent TN26 3TB
Printed in England by Intype London Ltd

A CIP record for this book
is available from the British Library

ISBN 0–571–20065–6

2 4 6 8 10 9 7 5 3 1

Characters

Gigi a woman, aged 50

Mimi her twin sister

The twins are not identical. They are the only and cherished offspring of average middle-class parents, now dead of natural causes. In Act One both have black hair cut in a fringe and straight bob, Chinese style; they are dressed alike and this creates an impression of strangeness. In Act Two they appear to be unremarkable with an ordinary family likeness.

The action takes place at the present time in the attic of their family home on the last day of their occupation.

Act One

Early morning. Dark. The twins are asleep.

A radio alarm clock sounds: Gigi wakes, turns the music low and switches on a lamp. Gigi stands at the side of Mimi's bed, holding a pillow. Mimi seems to be asleep.

Gigi Sometimes at break of day before you wake, there is a blissful silence. No prattle. An absence of strife. Me, myself, hardly there at all. I press my head into the pillow to feel my own life, throbbing. My heart. I get up to fill the kettle: my own thirst makes me. Mine. The air clasps me like a cold embrace. A drop of water in the eye of the sink winks at me. Me. Me. I eat a crust quietly to keep you asleep. Mimi?

Gigi puts the pillow back on her own bed. Then she draws back a curtain, behind which (under the eaves) are stacked cardboard boxes and packing cases. She pulls out a big box labelled SELL. *She takes a cloth-covered bundle from the top of this box, and looks round for another hiding place.*

Mimi wriggles and giggles, luxuriating as she wakes. Caught, Gigi thrusts the bundle back into the box. She pulls out another box, marked BEDDING. *She hastily strips her own bed, and stuffs the pillow, sheet and quilt into the bedding box. Then she unbolts the door and goes, putting a warning finger to her lips.*

Mimi waits, then peeps, then creeps a hand to the radio and turns up the volume. She rises to her feet and dances with dreamy delight. Then she suddenly drops down on the bed and lies flat.

Gigi comes with tea and toast. Vexed, she turns the music down low. Then she lies down on her own bed. In slow motion to the music they exercise, first left legs raised and pointing, then right legs. After five lifts of each leg, they lie still, breathing.

Mimi Is it today? Gigi?

Gigi (*brusque*) I don't know. Legs again

They repeat the exercises again faster.

Mimi Is it?

Gigi Mimi, I said: I don't know!

Mimi But you've already started.

Gigi Obviously we've got to get started.

Mimi Says you.

Gigi It's my say. Remember your promise? You have to do what I say. Or else. (*repeat routine of legs in silence*) Exercise! If we exercise, we don't need to go out –

Mimi Din-dins?

Gigi Of course. If you'd let me finish, I would have said we don't need to go out every day. It's too risky – coming in and going out.

Mimi (*flexing*) Legs.

Gigi Enough! Now, roll over. Back.

The radio stops playing and the lamp goes off.

Mimi (*intrigued*) Whoops! Gone.

Troubled, Gigi tries light switches.

Gigi (*confirming*) Gone.

She opens curtains at the window.

Mimi Dark!

Gigi (*soothing*) Hold on!

Gigi finds and lights a candle.

Mimi (*gazing at candle*) Pretty!

Gigi Mustn't let it burn long. We'll need it tonight.

Mimi Will it come back? The light?

Gigi No – not unless we pay. I was counting on at least another day. (*checking letters*) Bills. Bills. Bills. See? We've had three red reminders. (*to herself*) Now what do I do?

Mimi Talk-talk?

Gigi I did talk. The girl had a voice like cut glass – cheap and sharp: Customer Services. Told me to make an arrangement to pay off the arrears. Five weeks ago. I marked it on the calendar. There ought to be a law against putting people in the dark. No light. No heat.

Mimi No music.

Gigi (*snapping*) If we can't cook, we can't eat – not proper food. You'd better enjoy your tea, because I can't make any more hot drinks.

Mimi (*reaching for pot*) Tea for two?

Gigi Two for tea.

Mimi (*sulking*) My turn to play mother.

Gigi My turn today.

Mimi You're in a bad mood.

Gigi No milk. No sugar. Nothing left.

Mimi So what are we going to do?

Gigi I don't know.

Mimi But you've already started.

Gigi Because it's just a question of time.

Mimi But if it's not today, we needn't do anything. Yet.

Gigi (*scathing*) If it's not today! I never said that. Don't put words in my mouth. How would I know? You don't go round asking. Just in case it jogs their memory and they pounce.

Mimi Do they know we've been cut off?

Gigi What? Who? No. They're not working together, but they're all converging on us at the same time. Bound to when cheques bounce. Anyway, we can't live without power, so we've got to make a move one way –

Mimi (*with meaning*) Or the other.

They look at each other in silence.

Gigi (*inspired*) Unless –

Gigi pulls paper and rags out of the chimney.

Mimi You're making a mess.

Gigi I'm making a fire.

Mimi Up here?

Gigi Down there we might be waylaid. Pass me those bills in the folder that says unpaid.

Mimi Daddy used to make roly-poly knots with news-papers.

Gigi spreads out a sheet of newspaper, and attracted by a headline begins to read.

Gigi (*struck*) You begin to see why people root about in bins, grubbing up papers out of gutters. They're not just looking for half-eaten buns; they're hungry for news.

Mimi (*eagerly*) Light?

Gigi In a minute.

Mimi Let me!

Gigi Don't snatch. We can't afford to waste a single match. They burn their doors and floor-boards.

Mimi Who?

Gigi (*impatient*) People! People who can't pay. Once you find yourself in their shoes, it makes sense. You get cold. You want to eat. You need heat. So what do you do? You start consuming anything that comes to hand. Bit by bit we could eat the whole house – like termites. They'd arrive to take possession and there'd be nothing left. (*grappling with a chair*) The only problem is I'm going to have to take a course in demolition first.

Mimi grabs the chair, bashes it on the floor and it disintegrates.

Mimi Easy-peasy!

Gigi (*snatching*) I said no noise! We won't light it now. They might see the smoke. That would be a dead give-way. But we'll have another go tonight. If we're still here. (*brisk*) Now what?

Mimi Go walkies?

Gigi Stop that.

Mimi Stop what?

Gigi Being a baby. We need a plan.

Mimi What plan?

Gigi If I knew what plan I wouldn't be saying we need a plan. I'd say: listen to this plan. I'd be cheerful. Chirpy.

Mimi Like a tweet-tweet.

Gigi I said stop that!

Mimi (*excited*) Talk-talk.

Gigi puts a hand over Mimi's mouth.

Gigi Just stop that now. Sit up and sip nicely like a lady. We're not playing Lady-Baby. We're both going to be grown up. Today is going to be different. No mess!

Mimi Today is always different. You're always changing the rules. Chopping and changing so you can stay in charge. It was just the same yesterday. And when we were children. You were always the boss.

Gigi Today is different: our last chance to get it right.

Mimi So it is today?

Gigi I don't know. I meant if. If –

Mimi Well, what are we going to do? If.

Gigi I don't know – yet.

Mimi When will you know?

Gigi When I've had time to think. Now we've got no radio, we'd better keep track. Time check. What time is it?

Mimi (*echo*) What time is it, Mr Wolf?

Gigi I said stop that!

Mimi Why do you always have to be so purposeful? Why can't we play?

Gigi Because . . . I say. (*with decision*) So. You'd better get up now and put on your robe. We've got to keep warm. Come on. Get up.

Mimi Uppigetti!

Gigi (*fuming*) I said –

Mimi (*springing up*) Sorry! No more talk-talk.

They tie each other's sashes on kimonos.

Gigi Sash.

Mimi (*admiring sash*) Pretty.

Gigi Apricot.

Mimi Peach.

Gigi No. Apricot. Apricot has more depth.

Mimi Plum! Pineapple! Banana!

Gigi Now you're just being divergent. It's pink – not yellow. Pink. We're talking colour, not food.

Mimi Why can't it be both?

Gigi It can – but only if it works on both levels.

Mimi All right then. Salmon. Salmon pink. Tinned salmon.

Gigi Sounds horrible. Reminds me of Grandma's knickers.

Mimi Knicker legs!

Gigi Bloomers! Great bulging bloomers with elastic in the legs. All fluffy inside.

Mimi What happened to Grandma? She was nice.

Gigi She died, didn't she?

Mimi (*offended*) I know that, Gigi. I'm not stupid. I mean what happened to her after she died? Do you think she went to heaven? Is she an angel now? Or is it all lies? Is she just asleep?

Gigi (*crossly*) How can you be asleep with no eyes? If she's dead and burnt, she's got no body. Anyway, you only ask questions for the sake of it – to keep us talking. Kids used to do it in the classroom. I'd pretend to fall for it every time. Well, you were their friend, when they were talking. As soon as you said work, they were your enemies.

Mimi (*panicky*) You won't go back?

Gigi I can't go back. I did a deal. I needed the lump sum. I didn't altogether mind packing in work: I'd lost the knack.

Gigi strips Mimi's bed and puts bedding in a cardboard box marked BED.

Mimi Work is not all it's cracked up to be. Getting up and going out in the cold. Like today. It's nasty out. Raining.

Gigi (*decisive*) We need food, so we'll have to go out. We'll have to wrap up warm. We'd better hurry before they get here. If they caught us as we were leaving the house, we'd have no chance.

Mimi goes back to her bed and flops down. She rolls up her sash and cradles it like a baby.

Mimi 'Morning, Baby. (*baby voice*) 'Morning, Mimi. (*Gigi voice*) Nasty day – raining and cold. Baby can't go walkies in the rain.

Gigi Look! You can stay in. But I'm going out. I've got to get us something to eat. And some more candles. Which means I've got to sell something first. List.

Mimi (*shivering*) If it's today –

Gigi Yes. If they came while I was out, you'd be on your own. That's true.

Mimi What would I do?

Gigi What wouldn't you do?

Mimi I wouldn't answer the door.

Gigi If you moved – if you even breathed, they'd never go away. I'd be out. You'd be in. And you'd be trapped inside. Best come with me.

Mimi But it's raining.

Gigi Yes.

Mimi They might come while we were both out.

Gigi Then we'd both be out on our necks in the cold and the wet. That's why we need a plan.

Mimi We need a brolly. To keep the rain from running down our pretty little necks. Daddy said.

Gigi Don't be silly. Out on our necks is just an expression. Or is it ears? Why ears? Why not legs? Or backs? Anyway, we've got a brolly. (*looking*) Somewhere. If you want to stay, you stay. You can make yourself useful. You can carry on packing. But do it so we can find things again. It's all organised. I've just got to sort out a van.

Mimi When?

Gigi If. Maybe I'd better just look in the yellow pages now – in case . . .

Mimi We could go on a brum-brum.

Gigi (*scathing*) You can't move house by bus.

Mimi (*pained*) I meant when we go out shopping instead of walking and getting wet.

Gigi To do anything we've got to have money. All roads lead in the same direction. Money is the unholy grail.

Mimi (*inspired*) We could get some money out of a hole in the wall.

Gigi The hole in the wall won't give us any more money. Are you listening to me? We have no money. If they take the house today and turn us out in the street, what's going to happen to us? Well? We'll be just left, standing –

Mimi We could go indoors and sit down somewhere – sit on a seat.

Gigi (*derisive*) What seat?

Mimi A cinema seat.

Gigi With no money?

Mimi A free seat. (*inspired*) We could go to the library? (*Helpless, Gigi shakes head.*) The park. The swing park.

Gigi (*loud*) Dog dirt! Stinky bins! Mean boys!

Mimi (*soft*) Tulips. Puppy dog faces.

Gigi (*fuming*) There are no pansies in winter. No flowers at all. Only dead things. Brown leaves. Squashed worms.

Mimi Ducks. (*very soft, cajoling*) Quack-quack.

Gigi Don't! You're distracting me. We're not just going out for an outing. Quite the reverse: we're looking for another bolt-hole. Like a pair of blind mice. We're stumped for somewhere to go.

Mimi (*offering tea-pot, coaxing*) 'Nother tumpy-tumpy?

Gigi (*softening, but preoccupied*) Say cup of tea! Thank you, but madame does not require another cup of tea. Eat your toast. Let me concentrate now. I've got to find a van.

Mimi Two for toast!

Gigi searches through the yellow pages.

Gigi That could be the last toast finger you ever eat! Chew it well or you'll choke. (*reading*) Van. Commercial Vehicle Hire. See also Contract Leasing. (*marvelling*) Pages and pages.

Mimi Pages and pages. Pages and pages. Pages and pages.

Gigi (*irked*) No gabby gobby.

Mimi (*pert*) Sorry I spoke!

Gigi You don't want to get a crumb down the wrong throat-hole. Besides every time you talk you miss a bite. Gobble up. Then talk. (*reading*) Varnish. Vault. Vegetable. Vending. Self-drive? No, that's no good. We need a driver.

Mimi You drive.

Gigi No. I've lost my nerve. You need verve to drive a van. Otherwise you keel over on corners. It's got to be a proper removal van – with a man. Or two.

Mimi One for me and one for you?

Gigi (*ignoring this*) Right. I'm ready. Research is the order of the day. Action stations.

Gigi picks up the receiver.

Mimi (*snatching*) Me!

Mimi takes the list and carefully punches in the first number, then gives the receiver back to Gigi.

Mimi The phone's gone dead.

Gigi (*shocked, checking*) That means we've been excommunicated. I thought we were allowed grace days. Where did I put the bill? Blast! (*checking dates while Mimi plays with the phone.*) Leave the phone alone!

It won't work. We'll have to use a call-box. I'll need change.

Mimi (*accusing*) You said we've got no money.

Gigi I meant hardly any money. Don't be so counter-suggestive. You only do it to spite me.

    Gigi checks purse. Mimi goes to the window and begins to chant, low at first, then louder.

Mimi Rain, rain go away, come again another day. Rain, rain . . .

Gigi You're right though: call boxes eat money. So I ought to find a company near enough to walk there. Then I can call in person.

Mimi (*louder*) Rain, rain . . .

Gigi Walker and Willis. I know where that is. Could I walk three miles?

Mimi (*louder still*) Rain, rain . . .

Gigi What if it's closed?

Mimi (*very loud*) Rain, rain . . .

Gigi (*exploding*) You promised!

Mimi What if it's closed?

Gigi I'd just have to wait. But if it was open, I'd walk in and I'd ring the bell and I'd say: I want to book a van.

Mimi There may not be a bell.

Gigi You haven't eaten your toast.

Mimi Dry toast is not very. If we had any eggs we could dip in.

Gigi Look, Mimi. Don't keep demanding. (*showing purse*) See? At present – as of now – for today – this one single solitary day – I've got just enough for bread.

Mimi (*grabbing*) Me!

Gigi No!

Mimi snatches the purse. She takes out a Giro and waves it in triumph, bouncing on the bed.

Mimi (*sing-song*) Giro!

Gigi ignores this performance. She begins to tidy away the breakfast things into a box.

Gigi (*patient*) Please, Mimi. Let's not pretend. Give Gigi the purse. We're getting too old for these baby games. So give me the purse now, there's a good old stick. I'm not cross. Look, I'm smiling. I might even buy you some nice sweeties if we do go out. Please? They only give us just enough to survive. If we want anything else, I've got to sell something. And I've already sold just about everything that has any value – except the furniture. And the furniture is not antique. It's just old.

Mimi (*cradling purse*) My turn to play mother. Share and share alike Daddy said.

Gigi (*taking purse*) Daddy's dead. (*coaxing*) Come on. We've got to get dressed. You want to look your best. If they come again today, if they catch us unawares, if they manage to serve notice on us, they won't wait for you to get ready; they'll just knock once and then they'll batter down the door.

Gigi rummages in a box marked CLOTHES.

Mimi (*excited*) Will they really batter down the door?

Gigi Sometimes I could really give you a battering!

Mimi (*contrite, not scared*) Sorry. Gigi love Mimi?

Gigi Of course. Come on now. (*searching*) Find a pretty dress.

Mimi (*thrilled*) Will they be men?

Gigi Yes.

Mimi Are you sure?

Gigi It's always men

Mimi Why?

Gigi Because they're bigger.

Mimi Daddy wasn't big. He was little. He was a little, teeny-weeny, incy-wincy shrimp. (*amending*) No, a prawn. Whiskery. Beady eyes.

Gigi Even when they're little, they're strong. They've got muscle. Brawn. That's why they fight: because they've got the wherewithal.

    Gigi attempts to ease one of the boxes to the door.
    Mimi does not try to help.

Mimi Daddy didn't fight.

Gigi Daddies don't fight their own offspring – in theory. He fought in the war: that's what men do.

Mimi (*reflectively*) He clattered me once or twice.

Gigi A clip round the ears. A little nip now and then. A little tap with claws drawn in. That's supposed to be normal. Keep you in line. People used to tell him to knock it out of you.

Mimi (*reminiscent*) I was a proper little handful.

Gigi Other people advised him to try and communicate. Poor Daddy, he was a rank amateur at getting his own way. They'd be much more – professional.

Mimi (*whispering*) What would they do?

Gigi If we resisted, I suppose they'd just strong-arm us into the street. (*snapping*) Oh! for heaven's sake. Gabby-gobby. Trap shut. I'm trying to salvage these things. I mean for all I know they might have a right to everything we think we own – not just the house – but every last stick and stone. That's why we need a plan.

Mimi What plan?

Gigi What to do. Where to go. Can't you see I'm desperate?

Mimi Sorry!

Gigi You're always sorry, but you never stop. You never remember and you never do anything right. You never help. If they do put us out, it's your fault. Find yourself a dress! You got us into this mess.

Mimi (*dangerous*) Me?

Gigi Yes.

Mimi By going on a spending spree?

Gigi Spending money we never had, so it wasn't ours to spend.

Mimi (*flat*) I don't do it any more.

Gigi I know.

Mimi I promised.

Gigi (*tired*) Yes.

Mimi (*dangerous again*) So why are you being mean to me.

Gigi (*in retreat*) I'm not being mean to you.

Mimi (*threatening*) If you're mean to me, I might be mean to you.

Gigi I'm sorry.

Mimi I promised.

Gigi They don't care about promises. We won't be able to say: we've turned over a new leaf so come back later and we promise to pay. They'll just say: too late. Besides it would be a lie. We can't pay.

Mimi Will they really batter down the door?

Gigi First they'll knock.

Gigi investigates the box marked SELL. *then she finds a trilby and puts it on, frowning.*

Mimi Knock. Knock. Who's there? How many?

Gigi Three. One in a suit and two in work-clothes. But only one knocks at the door. (*scowling horribly*) The one in the suit.

Mimi Why is he dressed up smart?

Gigi (*rummaging*) He's the important one because he's got the writ.

Mimi What's a writ?

Gigi A writ is something written. Yes, a legal letter telling us we've got to get out. (*playing the man*) OUT! It's so simple. Once they serve it on us, they can lock us out. It's called securing the property for the proper owners. OUT!

Mimi (*enthralled*) OUT! Then what? What next?

Gigi Mimi, you're doing it again, distracting me. (*taking hat off*) Let's get on. I'm trying to find something else worth selling.

Gigi tips out the box marked DADDY: *a hat, a suit of clothes, a fair-isle pullover, an album, documents.*

Mimi Daddy's things!

*While Gigi attempts to sort the things, Mimi finds
a hanger and arranges them in the shape of a man,
which she hangs from the rafters.*

Gigi Now what we want is something portable and
expendable.

Mimi (*rummaging*) He wants his briefcase.

*Gigi pulls out a document case, tips out the contents,
then throws the lot disgustedly in a box marked
DUMP. Mimi attaches the empty case to the arm of the
suit and admires the effect.*

Gigi Old insurance policies? Dump! Keep-sakes? Why
keep? If we don't keep anything we won't need a van.
I mean we've been up here for weeks. Have we ever
needed the sideboard? Did we ever even look at the
sideboard? I mean the world is full of people who have
never even seen a sideboard. What do you think?

She holds up an album.

Mimi (*helpful again*) Ip-dip-dip –

Gigi (*screaming*) I said: be quiet. (*recovering at once*)
Mimi, I'm trying to keep one ear on the door while I do
this job. Tell you what. You listen. Come on. Kneel
down here. Now, keep your ear to the ground and if you
hear a sound . . . In fact, sideboards have probably gone
completely out of fashion. We won't be able to sell it
even for a song. We'll end up having to pay to have it
taken away.

*Mimi kneels with her ear to the floor. Gigi continues
to pack things into boxes.*

Gigi The fact is we don't really need any of these things.

Mimi (*taking photo*) Mummy and Daddy?

Gigi Their wedding photo. Dead relations. Dump.

Mimi (*snatching*) Nice! Pretty! Keep!

Gigi (*removing the photo*) On the other hand the silver frame might fetch a price. Sell. (*harried*) It's amazing how little value things have got once they've been lived with for a while. We've got to get money.

> *Gigi puts the photo in a box marked* KEEP. *She puts the silver frame in a box marked* SELL. *She sweeps the rest of the photos into a box marked* DUMP. *Then she takes a German helmet from the* DADDY *box.*

Mimi Is it a toy? A prop?

Gigi No, it's real. Feel!

Mimi Heavy. If only it was worth its weight in gold . . .

Gigi When you're selling, it's worth what people want to pay. It's old.

Mimi How much?

Gigi Don't know. We'd have to take it to a shop. Can't get a valuer to come here.

> *Mimi puts the helmet on Gigi's head.*

Mimi (*whispering*) Knock. Knock. Who's there?

Gigi Open up!

Mimi (*scared*) Are you a soldier?

Gigi I shall fetch the law if you don't open this door.

Mimi Who's there?

Gigi Sh!

Mimi We could open it just a crack – and keep the chain on.

Gigi (*brusque*) Don't you ever dare!

Mimi Why not?

Gigi Because if it's open at all, it'll be fingers forced in: first the letter of the law, then the boot.

Mimi They can't break the chain.

Gigi Yes, they can – they've got great, big cutters with steel teeth. They come prepared. They've got ramming rods. Then it's door smashed open and men in.

Mimi Even the man in the smart suit?

Gigi Especially the man in the smart suit. He's the boss. He hides behind the others, but he'll be there – in his smart suit with his smile.

Mimi Is he a smiley friend?

Gigi Yesterday he might have been a friend. Friend Provident. Or Friend Prudential. A listening friend. A friend in need. But today he's coming to collect on his good deed.

Mimi If we keep very quiet . . .

Gigi We may beguile them for a while. They may leave it till another day. Or they may lie in wait. But in the end, whatever we do, they'll win.

Mimi I don't like this game.

Gigi (*irritated*) It's not a game. It's a war.

Mimi Win or lose? It's the same talk-talk.

Gigi Win or lose, war is not a game. People die.

They look at each other. Gigi takes off the helmet.

Mimi Are we going to die?

Gigi (*with decision*) No. Let's get on.

Mimi You said –

Gigi What? What did I say?

Mimi You said: everybody dies.

Gigi It's true. I meant yes.

Mimi (*dangerously*) You say one thing and you mean another.

Gigi No. I meant no, not now.

Mimi You said: it's just a question of time.

Gigi It is.

Mimi You said: when the time is right.

Gigi You remember?

Mimi Of course. When?

Gigi If. If.

Mimi What is if?

Gigi If is . . . ? Scrub that. Go back to where we were a minute ago. Their game-plan. Meaning strategy. They're trying to wear us down. As in war of attrition. They don't want a big drama: because, of course, if we decided to retaliate, it could escalate . . . They think that if they hold off long enough, we'll capitulate and go away very quietly and just fade away slowly – somewhere out of sight out of mind.

Mimi If.

Gigi But there is another way. In fact, there's more than one other way. There's what we talked about: the quick way. Remember?

Gigi takes the cloth-wrapped bundle out of the SELL *box. She goes to the window, looks out, checking. She places the bundle on the window-sill.*

Mimi The quick way?

Gigi The quick way is to wrap things up here and now.

Mimi (*looking at bundle*) You wrapped it up. I remember.

Gigi You remember your promise?

Mimi When?

Gigi If! It's not the inevitable end. But it is an option. The quick way is not the only way. Only if I say so. (*shifting focus, but not changing the subject*) We could get rid of it: there's a market for these old things. Military memorabilia. (*touching the bundle*). Side-arms fetch a better price than mere sideboards.

(*Reassuring*) Mimi, I'm merely thinking out loud. There are lots of people like us but when it comes to the show-down, we're always on our own. Next door and over the road and round the corner they'd all say the same. (*spiteful*) It's your own fault for getting in a muddle. Pay up or do without. You've got no right to pets and telly sets if you can't pay. That's what they'd say. You want me to spell it out again.

Mimi (*dangerous, covering ears*) No!

Gigi (*accusing, over Mimi's protests*) You kept buying things on hire purchase and not paying.

Mimi No . . . !

Gigi In the end they took you to court. What was I supposed to do?

Mimi   . . . No . . . !

Gigi Let you go to prison?

Mimi   . . . No . . . !

Gigi I kept borrowing to pay for your things. Things they took back anyway.

Mimi . . . No . . . !

Gigi And your fines. In the end I borrowed on the house. Except by then I only had half the house. He took the other half. (*slapping Mimi*) Stop that!

Mimi's protests stop. She laughs.

Mimi Husband.

Gigi He said he had a conjugal right to half the house or both of us – being the husband. I had to borrow thousands to get him off our back! Now it's their house and they won't let us stay.

Mimi (*sadly*) Nice things. All gone.

Gigi Yes, nice things all gone, but we still have to pay. A debt doesn't just go away. And it doesn't stay the same size. It gets bigger all the time. Once you've got it – it does it on its own – it multiplies – like a cancer. It takes over your life.

Mimi Poor Gigi. Don't cry. It's not the end of the world. Mummy said.

Gigi When you close your eyes, it is the end of the world. Mummy died. People get old. They get tumours and varicose veins. Their eyes ooze. There must be a million different ways of dying. How many people get to choose? Hardly any. But they all get to die in the end. Where was I?

Gigi picks up a cricket bat. Mimi bowls an invisible ball. Gigi makes as if to hit the ball, then drops the bat in digust.

That's why I can't think. You get inside my head. I wasn't playing cricket. One can't just do nothing.

Mimi Two can do nothing. It's easy.

Gigi But doing anything at all depends on doing something else first. And meanwhile we have to eat. So whatever happens we have to sell something. Help me find something. What about the toys? This doll? This book? This bell? DUMP or SELL?

Mimi (*frantic*) No! KEEP! KEEP! KEEP!

Mimi drags the toy box away from Gigi.

Gigi (*soothing*) All right – you do that! You just keep busy: you pack and sort. This is my thought: we may just decide to stay here and hold the fort. We could become a media event. SISTERS UNDER SEIGE. TWINS STAND FIRM. Once you're on television, the rules change. You become a cause. People send parcels of food. Soft toys. Wreaths of roses. They'd watch with bated breath. They'd take sides. They'd see us being dragged out with draggled hair . . . I'll go and get supplies.

Mimi What if they come when you're out?

Gigi But we have to eat, and you won't come out in the rain.

Mimi (*panic*) You can't leave me here on my own!

Gigi You want to starve? You want to turn into skin and bone? You want them to find us hanging on the back of the door, stinking like a pair of dead cats?

Mimi No! Who would find us? Would it be nice young men?

Gigi Men!

Mimi drapes a net curtain over her head.

Mimi (*pensive*) I've never had a man.

Gigi (*shuddering*) I have. Once.

Mimi You had a husband.

Gigi Once. Once was enough. He tried to rip us apart and when he couldn't he ripped me off instead.

Mimi picks out a red plastic replica gun with a box of feathered darts. she loads the gun with darts.

Mimi What happened?

Gigi You know what happened.

Mimi Talk-talk.

Gigi NO! (*Pause*) He made me choose, didn't he? And I chose you.

Mimi (*prodding Gigi with gun*) Ip-dip-dip. My blue ship. Sailing on the water. Like a cup and saucer.

Gigi DON'T!

Mimi O.U.T. spells out. Out!

Gigi Don't!

Mimi What starts off little and wrinkled like a dear little winkle and grows huge?

Gigi Be quiet!

Mimi Was it as thin as a rolling pin?

Gigi You're being rude.

Mimi As tall as a telegraph pole?

Gigi It you don't stop being rude, I shall leave now.

Mimi (*firing at effigy of Daddy*) Why?

Gigi You know why.

Mimi Why?

Gigi You know the answers to all the questions.

Mimi (*firing repeatedly*) Why? Why? Why? Why? Why? Why don't we have a thing?

Gigi (*cold*) That's it! I'm going to go.

Mimi (*pointing toy gun*) NO!

Gigi Drop it! Now! (*Mimi drops the toy gun on the floor*) In the box, I said.

Mimi Didn't –

Gigi Did –

Mimi Didn't. Didn't. Didn't.

Gigi I didn't say it, but I meant it. I meant to say in the box. Satisfied?

Fuming, Mimi tips out the contents of the box.

Mimi Don't patronise me.

Gigi All right. I give up. Let's do nothing.

Gigi drops down on her knees, and lies curled, inert, unresponding. Nonplussed, Mimi watches.

Mimi Let's begin again. (*no response from Gigi*) Please? (*panic*) Please? Please? Please?

Gigi All right. We'll begin again.

Wearily Gigi crawls back onto her bed. Mimi copies her. Mimi waggles a leg, but Gigi lies, inert. Mimi fetches glasses of water and toothbrushes.

Mimi (*soft*) Surprise!

Gigi (*dour*) Very good! So? Surprise me again! Bring me a miracle.

Gigi lies, doing nothing. Mimi hugs Gigi. Comforting.

Mimi Mimi loves Gigi.

Gigi I'm sorry. It's just that we can't carry on like this. We can't not eat. It's too slow. It takes too long. We have to decide what to do.

Mimi (*eager*) Shopping? Together. When it stops raining.

Gigi No, not just shopping. If we go, we go right away from here. I don't mean just for today. I mean for ever.

Mimi Go where?

Gigi (*despairing*) Where can we go? I mean if we want to keep the right to squander the rest of our lives. We're stuck. We can't stay and we can't just go. We'd have to go and get help. That's the hard part.

Mimi (*cradling Gigi*) Baby go sea-side.

Gigi No. Too cold.

Mimi Girlie go school.

Gigi Too old.

Mimi Lady go open legs. Get man. Go beddie byes. Nice and warm. Feather bed! Once upon a time. Happy ever after.

Gigi (*freeing herself*) If you ever do that again, I shall leave you!

Mimi I've never had a man!

Gigi Liar!

Mimi (*cheerfully*) Tushy pegs.

They brush their teeth, facing, mirror-images.

Gigi (*correcting*) Teeth!

Mimi Gabby-gobby.

Gigi No more talk-talk. Come on, quick. We don't want them to see us in our see-throughs. Spit. Don't swallow. There. Show me your pearly gates? Good. Now we'll get dressed. Then we'll go out. We'll sell the silver. We'll get money. We'll find out where to get help.

Mimi (*looking*) Still too wet. (*adamant*) Can't go getting wet. Rain, rain, go away, come again another day.

Gigi (*desperate*) It's only drizzling. It won't hurt you. It's only water. If we get wet, I'll make a fire and then we'll get dry.

Mimi What if they come while we're out?

Gigi We'll get back in somehow. We'll become squatters in our own house. We'll climb over the alley fence and sneak in through the back cellar. And maybe there'll be bricked-up doors and barbed wires and we'll get torn and bits of rust will get in our bloodstream and that will be the iron in the soul. I'm going out. If you stay here, you'll be on your own.

Mimi (*panicky*) No!

Gigi (*soothing*) All right! We'll pack a bit more first, but I warn you, I'm going soon.

Together they pick up and pack away the stuff.

Mimi (*grumbling*) You're supposed to be the mother. I'm the baby. You're not allowed to leave me on my own. It's against the rules.

Gigi If they come, you'll have to cope alone. They might take you for a ride, stuff you in a bin bag full of holes and drop you in the river. Then you'd be wetter than ever.

Mimi (*laughing*) That's not true! You think they're really evil?

Gigi No. Yes. It depends. They're just – functionaries. Bailiffs.

Mimi Bailiffs?

Gigi People who do dirty jobs for other people – like servants.

Mimi Grandma was a servant, but she never turned anybody out of doors: she gave bread to beggars who came knocking. She said.

Gigi There are servants and servants. You have to be nasty to want to earn a living putting people on the street. Nasty men.

Mimi Nasty puddings.

Gigi It's just a job to them. They work for a company. A name. A name on a name plate. It might be a name on a door. A name on a store. Or a bank.

Mimi (*sad*) They won't give us any more money.

Gigi (*irritable*) Banks only give you what was yours in the first place. You have to keep in the blue.

Mimi (*fingering kimono, puzzled*) Blue? Why blue, Gigi? Blue is nice. (*reminiscent*) Once upon a time we had a blue television standing on one foot – like a mushroom with a shiny stalk. Lovely.

Gigi You have to keep on the right side. Otherwise they get you and they never let go.

Mimi If you make a mistake, it gets your ankles when you walk on the crack. It pulls you down into the gutter. It cuts your throat. It makes you into mincemeat. It serves you up for pies. Blood pudding pies. Full of mangled eyes and little gobs of fat.

Gigi Mimi, listen to me. When I asked you not to go in shops, buying things, you promised, remember?

Mimi What happened to the blue television, Gigi?

Gigi They took it back.

Mimi Do you think they sold it to somebody else or did they just dump it?

Gigi That's irrelevant! You promised not to do it again.

Mimi A promise is like a magic spell. If you break it something bad happens.

Gigi (*dry*) That's the theory. Do you remember you made me another promise.

Mimi I did. I do.

Gigi You promised that you wouldn't make another deal without my say-so.

Mimi Talk-talk?

Gigi That promise about not doing things implied that you would do other things.

Mimi (*sharp*) What things?

Gigi Whatever. For instance, if I ask you to be quiet when they knock at the door –

Mimi (*glib*) I promise.

Gigi That was one example. If I ask you to come with me, you're supposed to come. But you don't – even when you give your word.

Mimi If I give you my word, does it mean I've got to come?

Gigi Yes!

Mimi Then I won't promise.

Gigi You've got to promise.

Mimi Why?

Gigi Why?

Mimi Give me a reason.

Gigi Because I know best.

Mimi Says you!

Gigi Please!

Mimi Can we get another dog?

Gigi Please!

Mimi (*negotiating*) A dog?

Gigi (*resigned*) All right. A dog. Now promise.

Mimi Promise.

Gigi Show me your hands. No fingers crossed? Now promise again.

Mimi Promise.

Gigi Whatever I say, you obey me. Get it? Whatever I say.

Mimi Gabby-gobby? Talk-talk?

Gigi Yes, talk-talk. If they come today, whatever I say, you obey. Tomorrow the same. The next day the same. A broken promise is bad news. Dead bad.

Mimi Mummy died, Daddy died. Grandad died. Grandma died. Gramps died. Nana died.

Gigi That's different, because they didn't promise to live forever.

Mimi Mummy said I broke her heart.

Gigi It isn't always broken promises that make people die.

Mimi Will you die, if I break my promise to you?

Gigi (*hesitating*) No. But if I have to get help, they might make me go away.

Mimi He made you go away. Husband.

Gigi But I came back, didn't I? When they died, I came back to be with you. He wanted me to sell up and go right away. He wouldn't stay. He said: two is more than I bargained for, but when one of the two is not biddable, it's double-trouble. So he went. He took half the house.

Mimi He took the car.

Gigi It was his car.

Mimi I liked the car.

Gigi I know.

Mimi He did it to me in the car.

Gigi I know.

Mimi I didn't mind.

Gigi I did.

Mimi I know. You told him to go.

Gigi If he'd stayed, I'd have slit his throat when he was sleeping.

Mimi Would you?

Gigi No. But I'd have wanted to.

Mimi (*whispering*) You could have blown a hole in his head.

Gigi Shush!

Mimi You said!

Gigi I told you: I wanted him dead, but I couldn't do it.

Mimi I could.

Gigi (*quick*) But only if I said. And I said no. I let him go.

Mimi He went. He was afraid.

Gigi Not really. He knew I could never do it. Knowing me, he knew it was all talk.

Mimi I could. But you wrapped it up. You said it was sold, but I knew where it was hidden. You kept moving it around. In the bag. Under the bed. In the box. Now it's waiting for your say-so. On the window sill.

Gigi I may sell it today.

Mimi You said we should find a wishing-well and wish it to hell.

Gigi stands still, staring at Mimi, who smiles.

You see? I remember everything. I'm your best twin.

Mirror-images, they stare at each other.

Gigi (*firm*) Enough! There's no more hot water, so we won't bother with a proper wash. Just a cat-lick. (*using face-cloths*) There. Now we'll get dressed. That's next on the list. And then we'll put our faces on and our best foot forward.

They turn back to back, and dress inside the robes.

Mimi No looking! It's rude to look. He looked. He said: plump people look nice naked. Is it true?

Gigi It's a matter of taste.

Mimi He tasted me. He licked me all over. He gave my nipple a nibble. He bit me on the bottom. That was rude. But it was nice. You look nice. You look good enough to eat. Nice silky slip.

Gigi (*facing and stroking slips*) So do you.

Mimi I always buy two of everything. Or four. Or six. Or eight. Then it goes. Two into three won't go. Five. Seven. Nine.

Gigi (*impatient*) No wonder we're bankrupt: you never do anything by halves. You're a natural aristocrat. Or an aristocratic natural. You're a bit touched but you've got a touch of grandiosity. La grande dame. You should have been able to order things by the dozen and pay through the nose.

Mimi (*happily*) Mail order!

Gigi That too! We had everything. Catalogue companies. Credit cards. Telephone sales. Talk about Interflora. Things arriving in cellophane bags. Things being delivered in boxes on the back of vans. Trade-ins on old hoovers. Air-miles. Every offer was irresistible. Market penetration.

Mimi Talk-talk?

Gigi It means you get screwed.

Mimi You said that was rude.

Gigi When they saw you coming, they smiled. Wide smiles – like crocodiles! You were the perfect meal-ticket.

Mimi We. I didn't get the things for me on my own.

Gigi (*firmly*) It was your choice. I didn't want what you wanted. We're not the same person. We're not identical. We don't think alike. We don't even look alike. There's no need for all this copy-catting.

Mimi No more twin togs?

Gigi What does it matter now? We're twinned. Twined. Whatever it is that holds us together is like that invisible thread that unspools on river banks and winds round bird's feet so they can't fly away and they die. But before they die the thread twists tight and stops the circulation and the little scrawny legs swell up. And go bad. And then they drop off.

Facing each other, mirror-images, they dress.

Mimi You made that up.

Gigi Why would I make up a thing like that?

Mimi To make me sad.

Gigi (*urgent*) I just want you to resist temptation.

Mimi Poor little feet. Poor little tweet-tweet.

Gigi Stop that! We're not babies any more! We've reached the age of reason. (*slumping*) And yet – sometimes I still feel like a child. Fifty is not old. Some old people sail round the world. They leave their loved ones and cast off into the egotistical sublime. It's hard to believe I ever left this house. Once upon a time I had a life. I met a man and got married. It's not too late . . .

Mimi (*pulling up her skirt and flexing her abdomen*) Nice man?

Gigi (*furious, dragging Mimi's skirt down*) For God's sake!

Mimi (*hurt*) It was a joke.

Gigi How could I ever work with you on the loose? What was I supposed to do? Lock you in the cellar? Chain you up by the back door – like a bitch on heat? (*Mimi cries, quietly at first, then loud.*) All right, it was a joke. (*soothing*) Look at me. I'm laughing, see? Come on, now Kiss? Kiss-kiss. There! Let's do our hair. Uppigetti.

> *Mimi allows herself to be wooed. Facing each other, mirror images, they do each other's hair. They preen, then kiss.*

Mimi Kiss-kiss.

Gigi (*brisk*) Now. We go.

Mimi (*recoiling*) No. We'll get wet.

Gigi (*controlled*) Very well. We'll wait a bit. You sit. Look in your box. We'll kill some time. We'll wait for the rain. But we have to go soon.

Mimi How do you kill time?

Gigi (*preoccupied*) You can't really kill it – you only fill it.

Mimi How?

Gigi I make lists. If it doesn't stop in the next few minutes, I shall go. We have to eat. Correction: I have to eat. I'm hungry. (*writing heading*) List.

Mimi (*muted*) Eggs? Sweeties?

Gigi (*preoccupied*) A list of priorities.

Mimi Gigi! (*on a rising note*) Gi-gi-gi-gi-gi . . .

Gigi (*exhausted*) Please! Curl up in a corner. Suck your thumb. Stuff your skirt in your mouth. Silence yourself.

Mimi But –

Gigi (*harsh*) You promised.

Mimi (*quailing*) Sorry!

Mimi rolls herself into a ball, eyes closed. Gigi pins up a sheet of paper and finds a marker pen.

Gigi Basic needs. 1: Water. 2: Food. 3: Shelter. 4: Heat. 5: Clothes. (*A long pause.*) 6. A place. (*firm*) No, place is *not* the same as shelter. A shelter might be in one place – or it might be a moveable feast. Like a tent. Or a shell. If you happened to be a nomad. Or a mollusc. You know something? Cataloguing is an art – not an exact science. The possible permutations make the brain ache. You can take a leaf out of the yellow pages, and use the simple alphabetical, but you have to know what you're looking for. You have to be able give it a name. It doesn't say HELP anywhere in the book. (*no response from Mimi*) I said I've got brain ache. Meaning a pain in my head. (*still no response*) I mean water might be numero uno in terms of absolute importance, but you can always find a damp spot. If you've no cistern, it comes free. Pitter-pat. Like today. Well, most days. A trickle. If you stick your head in a culvert. Or a ditch between two lush green fields. And sometimes a flood plain. So, in terms of relative need, given your meteorological obsession – namely your rain mania, your phobia that is, a weather-proof roof is critical. So it's shelter first. Agreed? (*no response*) Then there's the whole question of higher level needs for which I need another list. I said I need another list. (*still no response*) I'm talking about spiritual needs now. (*strident*) Nutriment for the soul. Sights for the inner eye. Beauty and truth. Love. And stuff. What do you think? Can we take all that for granted or do we need to legislate? I mean – to conflate the two levels – if we just wanted to meditate – that is experience the so-called higher level at its highest level – couldn't we just crawl into their shelter, accept their charity, and wait for the mystic moment? (*no response*) You're allowed to answer. (*Silence.*) ANSWER ME! (*Silence.*) You promised to do as I say!

Mimi (*uncurling*) You were being mean to me.

Gigi I was simply trying to think.

Mimi Apologise?

Gigi I'm sorry.

Mimi Say I'm sorry I was mean.

Gigi I'm sorry I was mean.

Mimi Say Gigi loves Mimi.

Gigi Gigi loves Mimi.

Mimi Now hug!

They hug.

Gigi Listen, Mimi. Once you put a foot wrong you're on the slippery slope. It's downhill all the way. We've reached rock-bottom. But there is no rock-bottom. We're still falling. And it's dark. Nothing to hold onto – except each other.

Mimi has closed her eyes and is slowly revolving.

STOP THAT!

Mimi (*accusing*) You frightened me.

Gigi I frighten myself sometimes. Where were we?

Mimi We were waiting for it to stop raining. (*checking window*) It's stopped.

Gigi Yes.

Mimi Coats?

Gigi Yes.

They dress in identical coats.

Mimi That's it then. We go.

Gigi (*scared*) Yes. The future starts now. The bleak, blighted, benighted, roofless future.

Mimi You said if they lock us out, we'll get back in. Tonight.

Gigi That was talk-talk.

Mimi (*inspired*) Make-up?

Gigi No! (*relieved*) Yes. Let's put on our faces. If we decide to do it their way, and seek their help, we need to create a good impression. We need to look lady-like.

Mimi Who are they?

Gigi The helpers? Let's put it this way: help is the flip side of strip the flesh of your bones. Help or harm it's got to be other people.

Mimi What?

Gigi The hard thing is not knowing which is which.

Mirror-images, they make-up their faces.

Mimi Will we come back tonight?

Gigi We might.

Mimi You said –

Gigi I know what I said. It's called going round in circles getting nowhere in the end.

Mimi What about the things?

Gigi If they do – come today, we'll have left it too late. They'll just dump everything.

Mimi Where?

Gigi I don't know. Maybe they use the dealers that do House Clearance. See also under Antiques and Second Hand Furniture. But none of this is worth real money. What took us years to construct, they'll take apart – in next to time, for next to nothing. When all's said and done, it's only our history in a few cardboard boxes. We don't go back more than a generation or two. We've got no lineage, no heirlooms: our great grand-daddies are anybody's guess. They can dump the lot.

Mimi (*wailing*) No!

Gigi (*distracting Mimi*) But never mind that now. How do we look?

Mimi We look nice.

Gigi We look – odd.

Mimi Two is not odd. Two into two goes.

Gigi Two is one too many.

Mimi (*panicking*) You won't let them take me away?

Gigi A simple division? A split? I tried that, didn't I? Once. It's gone beyond that. We're stuck together. We're like a pantomime horse with two front ends. We don't fit the bill. We should go quickly now – before they come – just leave everything and go.

Mimi (*trotting*) Gee up, little horse!

Gigi But we can't just leave. You and me. Mimi and Gigi, we can't live in the open air. True, now and then people do take to the road. A few thousands. But, you and me, we can't do that. We're too fragile. We're neither here nor there. Don't you see what I'm trying to say: we haven't a chance of surviving on our own? We can't stay and we can't go – not just go – without a destination. Like it or not we're in their hands. We need to be part of something. It comes down to this: If we decide we don't want to co-operate in their fiction, we might have to do something desperate.

Mimi stops trotting and stares as Gigi finally unwraps the cloth-covered object, revealing a gun.

Mimi You said it should be sold.

Gigi I know what I said.

Mimi You said it could feed us for a week.

Gigi That was talk.

Mimi Talk-talk.

Gigi It may not work: it's old. It's just a souvenir. A collector's piece. Like an iron cross or a bit of shrapnel burnished to a shape. On the other hand (*checking*) it's loaded. If. It could speed us on our way. There'd be no home-coming. No trek across town knocking on closed doors.

Mimi If it works?

Gigi If. Daddy said it did.

Mimi Did he kill somebody?

Gigi (*quickly*) No. Poor Daddy! He got it for swapsies with his chocolate ration. He was on guard duty at the time. A hungry boy looming like a ghost out of the mist. Huge eyes pleading for food. A rat scavenging in the gutter. Daddy was so scared he pissed in his pants.

Mimi (*thrilled*) He never.

Gigi Mummy said. Remember their braided voices – one high, one low – at night in bed in the listening dark, sharing their secrets? Now we inherit their worst night-mares: fear food love death round and round like a sickening merry-go-round. I've tried . . . but I can't get it to stop. My heart. Your heart. Beating.

Mimi (*snatching*) My turn!

Gigi (*pointing the gun at Mimi*) Stand still!

Mimi (*unsure*) Gigi loves Mimi?

Gigi Of course.

Mimi (*panicking*) You want to get rid of me?

Gigi No! I only want to rest. I'm very tired. Shush! No talk-talk. Hold tight. No play now. No talk-talk. No bang-bang – not yet. In a minute we might change our minds and go for a trot. Flick through the yellow pages. Find the magic number. Unbolt the door. Kick over the traces and ride into the golden unknown.

Mimi (*loud*) Gee up, little horsey.

Gigi You remember your promise? Whatever I say, you obey. Like a good little horse.

Mimi Clip-clop!

There is a ring at the door, followed by loud knocking, then silence. They stand still, listening.

Gigi (*giving gun*) There. Now it's your turn. You do it for Gigi. First me, then you.

Mimi (*scared*) Mimi hug Gigi? Is it really the men?

Gigi Let's play it that way. When I say when.

Mimi (*checking*) If? Not when?

Gigi Whatever.

Mimi Does it hurt?

Gigi Probably.

Sings softly as they slowly swing round.

Horsey, horsey, don't you stop.
Just let your hooves go clippety clop.
Let your wheels go round.
And your tail go swish,
Giddy up, we're homeward bound.

Now, Mimi, now. Today is the day.

Blackout as the gun explodes twice in rapid succession.

Act Two

The clock radio plays. Mimi is asleep. Gigi comes with a breakfast tray. She moves softly, setting down the tray, tidying her own bed. She picks up a pillow and stands, watching Mimi sleep.

Gigi Sometimes at break of day before you wake, there is a blissful silence. No prattle. An absence of strife. Me, hardly there at all. I press my head into the pillow to feel my own life, throbbing. I get up to fill the kettle: my own thirst makes me. Mine. The air clasps me like a cold embrace. A drop of water in the eye of the sink winks at me. I am all and only me. I watch you smiling in your sleep.

Mimi wakes. The twins do not resemble each other and no attempt has been made on their part to achieve the look-alike.

Mimi You were talking to yourself.

Gigi I'm not myself.

Mimi (*arch*) Am I still Mimi?

Gigi That's something that doesn't change.

Mimi (*stroking*) Gigi! What do you mean 'not yourself'?

Gigi I need air.

Mimi Open the window.

Gigi I want to go out.

Mimi (*anxious*) What happened?

Gigi Nothing.

Mimi Was there a letter?

Gigi No. Nothing happened. I just woke up. Dressed. Went down. Got the tray. Came back. Spoke a few words. And here we are again.

Mimi What's that supposed to mean?

Gigi Don't ask!

Mimi Why?

Gigi Because you already know the answer.

Mimi Why?

Gigi Because we're twinned!

Mimi (*anxious*) What happened?

Gigi How should I know? A split cell. Something in the genes.

Mimi (*angry*) I mean what happened to you? I need to know.

Gigi Questions. Questions. That's something else that doesn't change. I used to believe that nurture was more important than nature, but now I know different. You've a stubborn streak. We were brought up the same way, so it must be in the chromosomes – the ones I didn't get. You're like a terrier hanging on to a trouser leg. Pro-grammed. I could kick you and you still wouldn't let go.

Mimi Because I still need to know.

Gigi Let's just say it's another day. Time is passing.

Mimi What has time got to do with anything?

Gigi That was just rhetoric. Time is a metaphor for life. You're too literal.

Mimi Why speak in riddles?

Gigi (*surprised*) I don't know. You're right though: plain speaking is best.

Mimi What has three legs and can't walk?

Gigi (*fuming*) We're not playing that game.

Mimi What has a tongue and can't talk?

Gigi A boot, of course.

Mimi Have you got a tongue?

Gigi Of course.

Mimi Are you a boot?

Gigi No.

Mimi So tell me in two words: what happened.

Gigi We've reached the nadir. How's that?

Mimi It's a bit fancy. But it's a start. Then what?

Gigi That's where we are now. Listen!

Mimi I am listening.

Gigi What do you hear?

Mimi Nothing.

Gigi That's right. It's so quiet in here. We could be a million miles away. A level silence. Listen again.

Mimi I am listening.

Gigi What do you hear?

Mimi The clock, ticking.

Gigi And again?

Mimi Twin hearts, beating.

Gigi That's right.

Mimi Me. (*Pause.*) And you. Like a time-bomb, ticking.

Gigi Listen again. (*opening window*) What else is there?

Mimi (*whispering*) The sound of distant traffic like a sea sighing.

Gigi (*soft*) Like an ocean pulsing against the shore. That's people pursuing their pursuits. And again? Listen once more.

Mimi Nothing.

Hushed, they stare at each other, listening to the clock and the heart-beat and the traffic, then they smile and hold each other. They rock with laughter. When they sober up again Gigi begins unobtrusively to strip her own bed, while Mimi eats.

Mimi Yum . . . mm . . . yum . . . mm . . . yum.

Gigi I wish you wouldn't do that.

Mimi Mummy said: eat properly – you're not a baby. (*cheery*) I'm a big girl now.

Gigi No. We're not starting that. We're not children. We're mature. (*wry*) That makes us sound like cheese. Yellowish. Rind wrinkled. Actually we're middle-aged. Practically old.

Mimi (*chortling*) We're not dead yet! Are we?

Gigi (*flat*) Don't ask stupid questions.

Mimi Are you mad at me?

Gigi No. I'm trying to concentrate. You're getting inside my head. Again.

Mimi (*chummy*) If we were dead, you'd be an angel.

Gigi (*dry*) Thank you.

Mimi (*munching*) This would be heaven. Is there a heaven?

Gigi You know the answer to that question. We've been here before.

Mimi Tell me anyway.

Gigi There is no life after death.

Mimi But we're not going to die yet?

Gigi No. We've got a lot to do first.

Mimi Today?

Gigi Yes.

Mimi What's the situation?

Gigi You know the situation.

Mimi I forget. (*flirting*) I do. You know it's not my fault. (*pat*) I suffer from short-term memory loss and poor sequencing. That's why I explode sometimes: frustration. It's your fault. You probably nudged me in the womb.

Gigi We're back where we started. Our own little room. My bed under the slanting roof so I can hear the rain. Yours under the window so you can watch the moon.

Mimi Nice. Cosy. Except they're dead.

Gigi Who?

Mimi Mummy and Daddy.

Gigi And the goldfish. And the rabbits. Etcetera. Our pets never lasted long. The fish got fungus and floated and the rabbits ran. Just like my man. My own little man. My one and only.

Mimi (*conspiratorial*) You sent him packing?

Gigi I asked him to go and he went. (*dry*) With alacrity.

Mimi With what?

Gigi Speed. He bolted – like the rabbits.

Mimi Run, rabbit, run, rabbit, run, run, run . . .
(*humming*) Then something about a gun. That's what
made him run.

Gigi Come to think of it he was a lot like a rabbit.
Randy and twitchy and timid all at the same time.

Mimi Poor Gigi. Mimi made Gigi sad. I'm sorry.

Gigi Don't be. I'm dry-eyed. It was already finished.
First he had a flutter and then a fling. He got more flam-
boyant. More flagrant, I should say. You were not the
first. I just decided to draw the line at sisters. Especially
twin sisters. Sisters are supposed to watch out for each
other. Otherwise it's all dog eat dog.

Mimi (*happily*) Woof-woof!

Gigi Don't start that!

Mimi They didn't put us out in the street?

Gigi Not yet. So you didn't forget?

Mimi Forget what?

Gigi Forget it! We're not going to keep going round in
circles. We're playing a different game.

Mimi What game?

Gigi It's called: FINDING A WAY FORWARD. Or KEEPING
TO THE STRAIT AND NARROW.

Mimi Tell me the rules.

Gigi I can't –

Mimi (*mocking*) Gigi doesn't know the rules?

Gigi (*gloomy*) When you start to formulate the rules, it's already too late.

Mimi They've been broken?

Gigi Well, yes. No. It's just that you learn them as you go along, so you're always in the wrong.

Mimi But there's always a next time. Another go? A shake? A turn round the board?

Gigi (*surprised*) Yes. (*reflecting*) Maybe. (*thinking again*) Probably not. (*definite*) The great thing is to keep going. We're not finished yet – not by a long chalk. Or do I mean stalk? To be honest, I can't tell you the rules because I'm still stumbling up against them all the time. That's part of the problem: you can't see what lies ahead and the edges are not very well defined. You'll have to frame yourself this time.

Mimi Are you trying to be mean? To me, I mean?

Gigi No. Just laying it on the line. That's rule number one: we tell the truth to each other. Otherwise it's no go.

Mimi (*puzzled*) Do we start now?

Gigi Whenever. (*correcting herself*) It's already begun.

Mimi Is it the weekend?

Gigi No.

Mimi Half-term?

Gigi No.

Mimi Christmas?

Gigi It doesn't matter what time of year it is – or day for that matter. When we're not part of anything.

Gigi takes the remnants of food away from Mimi.

Mimi (*relaxed*) Sounds good. What's going to happen?

Gigi It's not what happens. It's what we do.

Mimi Mimi and Gigi?

Gigi People.

Mimi Which people?

Gigi People who go under. Who haven't got the grit or the grip. Who give in to weak and wicked impulses and get pulled down by the current of forces beyond their control. Market trends. Interest rates. Abstractions. Population figures. Sounds statistical put like that. But the people are real: they start off as embryos curled up like caterpillars – cute maybe in their baby-grows – but later on they give you a sick feeling when you see them humped in doorways with their squalid dogs. Naturally I'd be different on my own.

Mimi How?

Gigi Higher up. More balanced, but more precarious. I see myself maybe looking down out of a window. I could decide to jump but I'd probably stay there, elbows on sill, popping up my chin, brooding, in control. Dog – if any – lapping clean water in a corner of the kitchen from a bowl marked DOG.

Mimi That's the third dog today.

Gigi I was bitten once by a miniature poodle. It sank its sharp little fangs into my wrist and nearly tore my hand off.

Mimi Was I there?

Gigi You were always there. Blood pooling on the concrete in the yard. You remember?

Mimi (*changing the subject*) Nobody got hurt?

Gigi No.

Mimi The stage was set, but nobody got hurt? Is that right?

Gigi Yes.

Mimi You said: now, Mimi, now.

Gigi I did.

Mimi But there was no big bang?

Gigi There were two big bangs, but no repercussions. Art is not life. A blackout could mean anything: it's not necessarily a catastrophe or a sudden end or even a change of scene. It could mean God winks. A symbolic eclipse. Or an actual power failure. Or a tiny absence of the faculty of thought. An electrical aberration in the brain. I needed the break.

Mimi Funny business. So what happened to the men?

Gigi There were no men – not then.

Mimi (*disappointed*) No men!

Gigi Let's say they just melted away.

Mimi Like clouds.

Gigi Like airy phantoms. Immaterial.

Mimi (*looking up at skylight*) Like clouds. (*singing*) Blue sky . . . nothing but blue sky. (*sharp*) They gave us another chance.

Gigi Yes. In due course, they'll be back – of course.

Mimi (*pouncing*) Who are they?

Gigi Please. Don't start.

Mimi How can I learn if you never tell me anything?

Gigi I'm trying to find a way forward. Truthfully. I want it to be different this time. If you keep forcing the issue, it will go the same way.

Mimi (*familiar*) Tell me a story.

Gigi (*anguished*) No. It's got to be different this time. They want it to be different.

Mimi Why?

Gigi They live in hope.

Mimi Who are they?

Gigi People.

Mimi Feeble people – like us?

Gigi Just people. The lot. Rich and poor. Paupers. Princes. Powers and principalities. The powers that be. (*very dry*) Our peers. You and me.

Mimi (*awed*) Are they here – the powers that be?

Gigi Suppose they are?

Mimi Watching our every move?

Gigi Of course. They wouldn't be here otherwise.

Mimi Why?

Gigi They want to see whether we can work it out.

Mimi Is it a puzzle?

Gigi Of course. Life is a puzzle. An enigma. A cryptogram without a key.

Mimi You always say of course.

Gigi Do I? Of course – that's because some things are obvious.

Mimi Not to me. Of course! It means you think I'm obtuse.

Gigi Not at all. You ask questions because you don't take anything at face value. Part of your mind got stuck at a certain stage. But damage carries compensatory advantages. It's a well-known fact that people like you are very perceptive.

Mimi People?

Gigi (*firm*) People!

Mimi Walls!

They look at each other and laugh.

Mimi Your turn?

Gigi We're not playing that game. There's no free association in this version. Everything has to be paid for in advance.

Mimi You take it for granted that you get to choose!

Gigi That's rich coming from you!

Mimi (*eagerly*) If we were rich –

Gigi (*firm*) But we're not ever going to be rich. Put that idea out of your mind. This time no extravagances. This time we're going to eke out an existence. We're going to learn from our experience. We're going to introduce budgetary controls.

Mimi (*shuddering*) How?

Gigi Discipline. That's what's needed. Get up!

Mimi No!

Gigi I'm up and dressed. I've tidied round. I've done the ground work. I've worked out a routine.

Mimi (*relieved*) You mean exercise?

Mimi slides out of the covers and flat on her back slowly waves her legs in the air like antennae. Gigi instantly grabs her bedding and folds it up.

Gigi No. I mean a way of coping with the real world. Exercise isn't an end in itself. It's supposed to be a preparation for life, not a substitute.

Mimi (*singing*) Up and down. Up and down.

Gigi Listen?

Mimi (*subsiding*) I am listening.

Gigi In the beginning we were starting from scratch. We muddled along. I needn't summarise. I needn't remind you it went wrong. We weren't equipped with whatever it takes. It got to the point where there was only one way out: and that was out.

Mimi (*echoing*) Out!

Gigi But as time goes on, things change. As time goes on, we learn. We don't stay the same. We've got hindsight.

Mimi (*exercising*) One, two, three, in; four, five, six, out –

Gigi For God's sake, Mimi, will you please just listen. I'm talking about learning from history. (*harsh*) History is a teacher. I was a teacher. But I was never in control. I lost out. I was out of step. I was tied to you. But we won't go into all that. Just trust me: I'm on your side. The way forward is to fit in. So we're fitting in. Then we won't be misfits any more. (*shouting*) Get up! On your feet!

Cowed, Mimi stands up and Gigi roughly strips off the sheet from her bed.

57

Mimi (*shivering*) I'm cold.

Gigi Do as you're told.

Mimi I did do.

Gigi Get up means get dressed. It doesn't mean stand up like bloody homo erectus. It means stand on your own two feet like homo sapiens. In other words use your brains.

Mimi I said I'm cold.

Gigi And I said: if you get dressed you won't be cold. (*throwing clothes at Mimi*) There's no allowance for fuel. That's not part of the deal. We can only survive by denying ourselves everything that's not free. We're not ever going to get cut off – if we're careful. Poor people and old people, people on pensions are supposed to be very rigorous with themselves. So get dressed. Now!

Mimi (*resisting*) Mummy said: wash first. (*hastily*) I know Mummy's dead.

> *Mimi cries softly as she gets dressed. Gigi draws back drapes and reveals the stack of big cardboard boxes. The boxes are already labelled:* KEEP, DUMP, SELL, *etc. Gigi begins to pack.*

Gigi (*rhythmic, quiet but firm*) Rule number one: tell the truth. Rule number two: think before you act. Rule number three: before you put a foot forward check with me – Get dressed!

Mimi Jibber-jabber! Talk-talk!

Gigi What's that supposed to mean?

Mimi Are you making the rules up as you go along?

Gigi I'm trying to create a better life.

Mimi (*muted*) Good.

Gigi Out of what we've not got.

Mimi (*unsure*) I see. Why are you packing? I thought we'd been given another chance.

Gigi We've been given another chance. A breathing space. But that's all. It's a space. But we've got to fill it, using our own resources.

Mimi (*singing uncertainly*) The air we breathe, the sky above . . . Then something about birds not working and grass growing green. And love. And lilies, I think.

While Gigi works and talks at speed. Mimi dresses and dawdles. Mimi admires herself: her legs, her shoulders, her face. She puts on make-up. She preens.

Gigi (*harsh*) You're talking about visions. Palliative crap. Food for thought. But that's all. It won't fill our bellies. We are not remotely like the lilies of the field or the lilies of the valley. We are what we are. Nothing's different. Your mind hasn't been modified. I'm not stronger. We haven't suddenly got more of whatever it takes to take us to the top. We're not charismatic. We're still near the bottom of the heap. Opportunity is not going to knock on our door and whisk us to celebrity. Once in a blue moon that happens to somebody, but we're on the wane. Our bric-a-brac is not hidden treasure. We've got nothing worth selling and it's too late to sell ourselves. A puff of star-dust is never going to transform our lives. No porn merchant is ever going to take a picture of our thighs and bellies to flash across a screen. Unless we gift our bodies to posterity, we have no value: eye-balls, hearts, kidneys, hidden bits.

Mimi (*giggling*) That's rude.

Gigi My rudeness – as you call it – is not gratuitous. I'm trying to make a point. The point is – are you listening?

Mimi You told me to get dressed. I look nice.

Gigi Well, anyway, I've forgotten the point. (*defeated*) Yes, you look very nice. But that's not the point. It's not what we are that counts, it's what we do. Get it? It's their game, but it's our move. If we bite the hand that feeds us, they cut it off – in a manner of speaking. The little itty-bitty dog was put down, remember?

Mimi (*frightened*) But who are they?

Gigi (*matter of fact*) People.

Mimi People? Again?

Gigi I keep telling you: there's nothing else.

Mimi Who said?

Gigi Who said what?

Mimi Who said we could stay? Who said we could try again?

Gigi They simply gave us time to pay . . . The courts, of course. (*faltering*) But the courts are only the outward and visible . . . (*impatient*) The tip of the iceberg.

Mimi What iceberg?

Gigi Oh! Mimi. What is an iceberg? An iceberg is just a figure of speech. For the purpose of elucidation an iceberg is an invisible mass. The courts preside, but the people decide. Therefore the people are the hidden mass. The people – as represented by the courts of law – have given us another chance. Satisfied? So help me. We're packing again.

> *Mimi seizes Gigi's hand and circles the palm with a finger, then tickles her under the arm.*

Mimi Round and round the garden like an apple pie. One step, two steps and tickle you under there.

Gigi Don't start that!

Mimi We're going round in circles. Again.

Gigi No, we're not – not this time. We're getting out of here.

Mimi (*challenging*) Good. It's nice and fine. The sun is shining. Let's go.

Gigi (*firm*) No. Not yet.

Gigi locks the door and holds the key.

Mimi I'll go on my own. (*trying door*) Key?

Gigi No key.

Mimi (*making a grab*) Mimi wants the key.

Laughing, they struggle over the key. When they pause for breath, Gigi still has the key.

Gigi No. Listen. Let me put you properly in the picture. We've got a future now. I'm your carer. That means we both get paid to stay alive, but I get paid an extra bit for looking after you.

Mimi Why? Why you? Why not me?

Gigi Because I did the business. I explored the avenues, climbed the stairs, knocked on doors, swallowed the free advice, talked up a storm; and managed to convince the powers that be –

Mimi Who?

Gigi Never mind who! We've been assessed. You're a special case – a case of special need. But I'm not really in charge because you're stronger than me: in other words we've got to agree. There's no government without consent. So there – take the key. Now we've got that straight, I'm going to finish packing.

Mimi (*teasing*) 'Bye, Baby Bunting . . .

Gigi All right. Go!

Mimi makes a grab for Gigi's handbag.

Mimi (*sing-song*) Giro!

Gigi Fine. Take it. (*Mimi takes purse.*) But this is your last chance. If you go now, you're on your own. I'll be gone when you get back.

Mimi (*teasing*) 'Bye!

Gigi tries to stop Mimi again. This time the tussle is not playful and Gigi is thrown back onto the bed.

Gigi All right. Take it. Go. Just remember, though. I'll be gone. There'll be no Gigi and no house. You won't need that key. There'll be new locks. Concrete blocks in the windows and doors. There'll be no getting back in.

Mimi But you said –

Gigi That's all right. You'll manage fine on your own. I can just see you tottering along with a dog, a moth-eaten blanket, and few carrier bags.

Mimi You said they'd given us a fresh start!

Gigi The point is: in reality you can't just begin again with a clean slate because they don't cancel everything out. You go on living like an old mule with everything you've already fucked up stuffed in a sack and tied to your back. If you show willing, they hand you out a hand out. In short –

Mimi They haven't let us off the hook? We're not free? We're still dangling? We're still in debt?

Gigi That's it. The fiscal problem is not solved – just shelved. We're supposed to stay solvent. Correction: we have to maintain an acceptable level of insolvency.

We won't be adding or subtracting anything, but we'll survive.

Mimi If I agree, we get to stay together? If I hand over the key – we get to stay alive?

Gigi And the purse. Then we'll both stay on the sunny side of the street – in a manner of speaking.

Mimi hands over the key and the purse. Gigi puts both into her pockets.

Mimi (*sharp*) So why are you packing?

Gigi (*evasive*) Come again?

Mimi The boxes are back.

Gigi Ah! Well . . . yes . . . we have to pack . . . of course.

Mimi You said: if I go, there'll be no Gigi and no house. Now you tell me we're leaving this house?

Gigi Yes. That's something we still have to do.

Mimi You said –

Gigi I said nothing about staying here.

Mimi You did. You said they said we could stay.

Gigi As in 'stay of execution'. A breathing space. A spell of time to keep us off the street. Of course we have to leave in the end: that's a given.

Mimi We're not coming back – not ever?

Gigi Never.

Mimi So there's no happily ever after for ever and ever amen?

Gigi No – not here. We have to go away from here. That's the condition. That's what we have to do.

Mimi No! Why can't we go back to the beginning?

Gigi Be born again? That's not an option.

Mimi Back to before it all went wrong?

Gigi Look, Mimi. It didn't went wrong. We did it wrong. So now we have to pay. We're not allowed to stay here. We don't own this house any more. We have to leave because it belongs to the bank. So we have to go. That's why I'm putting all our things in boxes. And you're going to help me. We've got to go.

Mimi (*wary*) When? Not if?

Gigi (*evasive*) Eventually. Soon. (*plunging in*) Dammit all, today!

Mimi So it's not different? It's just the same.

Gigi No. It's different.

Mimi How?

Gigi Because I say so.

Mimi (*with digust*) That's trickery. Jiggery-pokery.

Gigi Not at all. Don't you see? I've accepted our fate. My mind-set is different. That's a different state. Call it a state of grace. A graceful submission to a grateful state. A realisation.

Mimi The state is grateful?

Gigi Of course. Because we're not creating mayhem. We're not starting a riot. We're not starving in the gutter and getting the dribbly shits or spreading diseases or getting greedy and grabbing loaves off shelves. Come on. Let's get on. We're going to be late.

Mimi Today?

Gigi How many more times? Yes.

Mimi But we'll be together?

Gigi That's up to you. You have to co-operate.

Mimi They won't want us to separate? They won't tear us limb from limb?

Gigi No.

Mimi What if it rains?

Gigi It's not going to rain.

Mimi (*checking*) Blue sky.

Gigi That's right. Besides, we're not going to live in a cardboard box, so the wind and the rain won't matter to us. The boxes are only for our things till we get there. We'll take up residence in a nice little room with a door and a window and a floor. If we keep our noses clean, they'll pay to keep us quiet. After all, we'll be no trouble to anybody sitting in some hotel room with our hands folded gently in our laps, gazing out of the window, growing old. (*coaxing*) Come on. Help me to pick out a few keep-sakes.

> *Gigi is nervous now, but she continues to pack. She takes a photograph from the bedside table, wraps it in a cloth and places it in a box marked* KEEP.

Mimi Will it still be just you and me?

Gigi Yes.

Mimi Free to come and go? Not penned in? Not turned out? Free as air.

Gigi Nothing is really free, Mimi. Not even air. The air doesn't do its job on its own. We have to eat to breathe. We have to put something in to get something out. That's why – in the end – if we want to stay alive, we have to stay inside the fence, so that we can feed out of their trough.

Mimi (*beginning to get angry*) What fence?

Gigi The fence is like the iceberg. Oh! Shit. Some things are invisible, but it doesn't mean they're not real. When we leave here we'll go into a rented room. And they'll pay. And providing we don't put a foot wrong, they'll go on paying. The fence is their system. We'll be inside and providing we play by their rules, we really will be free – within limits. We won't be prisoners – not in that sense. You'll see.

Mimi I don't see!

Gigi For instance, we won't be able to go places, but we'll be able to think about going places. We won't be able to own a car, but we can watch other people driving along the road. We won't be allowed to touch, but we'll be able to look. The same thing is true of lots of people. Millions. They don't make a fuss. Sometimes you see them trailing meekly along dusty roads, going nowhere.

Mimi (*sullen*) You've decided we've got to go. It's your choice.

Gigi Yes. Of course. But only because that's the way it's got to be.

Mimi You won't fight to stay? We've always lived in this street.

Gigi No way!

Mimi (*wailing*) Why?

Gigi (*shouting*) How many more times? We're on our own, so we can't win. Staying is not an option – unless we're dead.

Mimi looks stunned and then, instead of putting things into the boxes, she begins to drag things out pell-mell, breaking, tearing, pulling down curtains,

dragging out wires in a monstrous temper tantrum.
Exhausted and scared, Gigi abandons the effort to
control the situation. Within seconds the order in the
room has been destroyed.

Mimi (*growling*) You think I want to? You think I like
it? You think I don't know? You think you can make
me? You think I don't know? You think this makes me
happy? You think . . . you think . . . you think . . .

Exhausted, panting, Mimi becomes quiescent. Gigi
watches, then warily approaches Mimi and puts out
a hand. Mimi smashes away the hand with incredible
ferocity and Gigi recoils to a safe distance.

Gigi Please . . .

Mimi You think I won't? You think I can't? You think
I don't want to? I do. You think you know everything
but you have no idea. You don't even begin to know.
Does your hand hurt? Is it bleeding? What I feel in my
little finger is a million million times worse than anything you could ever feel. You think I'm an idiot? You
are an idiot. You think you have a mind? You have no
mind. You think I like being tied to you? I hate it. You
think I love you? I hate you.

Gigi (*unnerved*) I'm sorry.

Mimi Don't be sorry.

Gigi (*involuntary*) I'm sorry.

Mimi (*threatening*) I said don't be sorry: sorry is no
good.

Gigi I meant I'm sorry I said I'm sorry.

Mimi You're so stupid.

Gigi I know.

Mimi Don't you understand anything? You're all I've got and you're so stupid. I've got nobody else. Don't you understand? You are the only thing I've got and you are nothing. What does that make me?

Gigi But –

Mimi But what? Go on. Say it. You know what you were going to say, so say it. Don't pretend you've forgotten.

Gigi I was only going to say it's the same for me.

Gigi cowers as this remark produces another storm of breakages.

Mimi Never . . . never . . . never . . . never say that again.

Gigi Please . . . don't do that.

Mimi Don't try to control me by pretending to be me. What did I just say?

Gigi I'm not trying to control you, I'm pleading with you.

Mimi You think I'm stupid?

Gigi No.

Mimi You think I'm stupid?

Gigi NO!

Mimi You said we'd always tell the truth. So I'm asking again. You think I'm stupid?

Gigi No.

Mimi Liar!

Gigi I think you're a genius.

Mimi Liar!

Gigi No. I mean it. It's just that the world isn't made for geniuses. It's a mad world.

Mimi And I am very very sane.

Gigi (*still scared*) Yes.

Mimi Why are you scared? Are you scared because you think I'm mad?

Gigi No.

Mimi Don't lie to me. Well? Answer me!

Gigi I don't like it when people lose control.

Mimi Correction: you don't like it when you lose control. I'm in control. Right?

Gigi Right.

Mimi If I were out of control, you'd be dead. Right?

Gigi I don't know.

Mimi Good. That's fine. I know you don't know. You're allowed to tell the truth. So now I'm telling you: if I were out of control, you'd be dead. Get it?

Gigi Yes.

Mimi Look out of the window. What do you see?

Gigi Nothing.

Mimi (*scathing*) Nothing?

Gigi (*scared*) Everything. Empty street. Windows.

Mimi Eyes. Watching.

Gigi Grass, trees, now and then a car, a toddler playing.

Mimi Come on. Come on.

Gigi (*with dread*) Houses.

Mimi Yes. Houses.

Gigi Please –

Mimi And where are we? Well?

Gigi Inside our house.

Mimi Again? Louder.

Gigi (*scared*) The point is it's not our house any more.

Mimi Why not?

Gigi Because –

Mimi What happened?

Gigi You know what happened.

Mimi Don't fuck me around.

Gigi Do you mean . . . ?

Mimi I'm asking the questions. Answer me.

Gigi But I was only going to ask –

Mimi Is it right to answer a question with a question? Is it polite?

Gigi No.

Mimi So give me an answer.

Gigi (*whispering*) I can't –

Mimi Why not?

Gigi I'm scared.

Mimi pulls Gigi to her feet.

Mimi All right. Now. I'm calm. I'm not going to hurt you. Now answer my question. You want me to repeat the question? See? I'm reading your mind. You're thinking you'd like to get away from me. Maybe you'll decide on a different scenario after all. You'd like to get rid of me. But you didn't, did you? You didn't kill me off. Or you. You wanted a happy ending. So what did happen?

Gigi Nothing.

Mimi Nothing?

Gigi Nothing.

Mimi Say it again – louder this time. So we can all hear . . .

Gigi Nothing happened.

Mimi Thank you. (*pouncing*) But what does that mean?

Gigi (*scared*) I don't know.

Mimi Yes, you do. Think?

Gigi I am thinking. We got to the point of no return?

Mimi Thank you. You said it was my fault. Was it my fault?

Gigi I don't know. (*scared*) Partly –

Mimi Did I make myself?

Gigi No.

Mimi Did I make the world?

Gigi No.

Mimi Am I God?

Gigi No.

Mimi Is there a God?

Gigi No.

Mimi (*furious*) Think again: is there a God?

Gigi I don't know.

Mimi That's better. Just testing. So is it my fault?

Gigi No.

Mimi Thank you. So simple when you tell the truth.

Gigi (*scared*) It's not that simple.

Mimi Isn't it?

Gigi If it were that simple we wouldn't be here.

Mimi Wouldn't we? And where would we be?

Gigi I don't know. The older I get the less I know.

Mimi (*breaking things again*) You think I want to hear that? You think that does any good? You think a person in agony want to hear that there's no cure? Do you know why I hate you? Because you think you know all the answers and you know nothing. Why do you think I want to stay here?

Gigi Because –

Mimi (*warning*) Think!

Gigi Because . . . in the beginning . . . when we began . . . we were born . . .

Mimi Why don't you admit you don't know the answer?

Gigi Because –

Mimi Think!

Gigi Is it because you identify your life with this place?

Mimi Don't talk crap! How can a person be a place?

Gigi Sorry!

Mimi Don't say sorry all the time. You're not sorry you insulted me. You're only sorry because you're sorry for yourself. You are a nothing. A zero. A void. A gaping hole. Me, I'm nothing. I've got you, so I've got nothing. Nothing. It's worse than nothing. Because nothing would be nothing. My carer? You? Me? Like a monkey on the end of string. Like a donkey in a field. Like a lunatic. You make me sick.

Racked, Mimi cries.

Gigi What can I do?

Mimi (*spent*) It's no good if you have to be told. You're supposed to be the one in the know. If you don't know, how can I know? If you can't work it out, if your logic won't do the trick, how can I be expected to grow? That's right. Even before we were born, you were feeding off me. Go on then. Speak.

Gigi You want the truth?

Mimi What did I just say?

Gigi Sometimes at the break of day –

Mimi Keep it simple. Just remember one thing. It's not about this place.

Gigi (*defeated*) No. Of course not.

Mimi (*fuming*) Don't pretend to understand. (*bitter*) What do you know?

Gigi Nothing.

Mimi Good. (*abrupt*) What is a place?

Gigi A place is . . . a place?

Mimi Try again.

Gigi A place is only a place?

Mimi So it's not about a place, is it? Is it? Does that make sense? Do you understand?

Gigi (*hesitant*) I think so.

Mimi Don't lie. Truth is a two-way street!

Gigi I don't understand.

Mimi Good. Now we're getting somewhere. When you know what you don't know, there's hope.

Gigi You won't leave this place?

Mimi It's not about this place. Or any place.

Gigi I see. (*relieved*) I see. I do see. It's not about a place. If it's not about a place, it's got to be about leaving. The act of leaving. It's about an action.

Mimi Right.

Gigi It's about a reason.

Mimi Right.

Gigi I see. I do see.

Mimi Say it!

Gigi (*scared*) You refuse to make a move without a reason – just because I say so. Is that right? It's about us, isn't it? You and me. Mimi and Gigi.

Mimi (*with immense calm*) I'm not a puppet. Or a parrot. You can't pull my strings or put words in my mouth.

Gigi It's not me! They're forcing us to do what we do.

Mimi (*scathing*) The powers that be! Do you still think I'm a fool? Do you think I don't know it's down to us? We decide. That doesn't just mean you – that means me too. All our lives – ever since we were born – you've been taking the words out of my mouth. Now it's my say. If I say we stay, we stay.

Gigi Sometimes –

Mimi Say it!

Gigi I despair. Because –

Mimi (*fierce*) Don't say any more.

Gigi But –

Mimi Just don't. (*abrupt*) How long have we got?

Gigi As long as it takes, I suppose.

Mimi Don't.

Gigi Don't what?

Mimi Just don't try any of you clever-clever rejoinders. (*scathing*) How long is a piece of string? Your talk-talk doesn't cut any icebergs. So how long have we got?

Gigi Not long.

Mimi How long is not long?

Gigi Today is the day. We need – If – When –

Mimi You don't need to talk: I can read your mind. You want to get on. You always want to get on. You want to clear up this mess. You want to pretend there's a purpose. Do it then.

Still scared, Gigi begins to tidy.

Gigi (*smiling warily*) Thank you.

As Mimi taunts her, Gigi continues to pack, picking up speed in spite of everything. Now and then she looks towards the window.

Mimi Look at you, packing! It's so easy to make you smile, but the smile is only mouth deep. It doesn't reach the eyes and behind the lips the teeth grind. Checking the window, are you? You think I don't know? I know everything. Do you know why you're obsessed by order? Because you're frightened of chaos. You're so stupid. Do you think boxes can box it in? Do you think filing it away can make it go away? Do you really believe pigeon-holes can hold anything except pigeons? So? What do you want to do with this stuff? These nick-nacks. (*scathing*) Make another list? Shouldn't we just junk it and bunk it?

Mimi picks up the box marked SELL *and tips out the contents.*

Gigi (*involuntary*) Don't – !

Mimi I warned you.

Gigi I wasn't trying to control you. I just meant: why tell me to pack up if you mean to undo everything I do. It doesn't make sense.

But Mimi is sorting through the scattered contents of the box, looking for the cloth-wrapped bundle. She drops the covers and examines the gun.

Mimi Doesn't this make sense?

Gigi Be careful with that thing!

Mimi You think I'm really thick? If I did it, it wouldn't be an accident, would it? What would it be?

Gigi An action.

Mimi That's right. Now we're getting somewhere. You're reading my mind. And I'm reading your mind: I see a glimmer of hidden hope. You want me to blow myself away.

Gigi No.

Mimi (*mocking*) No. No. No. Words are cheap! Is there nothing else on offer? No unbeatable bargains? Nothing on approval? No more trial runs? No absolute guarantee?

Gigi No!

Mimi Check the window.

Gigi stands, frozen.

Do it!

Gigi looks out.

Gigi (*relieved*) Not yet.

Mimi What do you see?

Gigi Nothing.

Mimi Nothing? (*looking*) Leafy tops. Birds on roof ridges. Houses two by two. Green verges a long way down. Someone stooping to steady a toddler stepping off a steep kerb.

Gigi (*urgent*) An ordinary day in a quiet street. Let's keep it that way.

Mimi (*taking aim*) I could take a pot shot at that child.

Gigi reacts so quickly to these words that she gets control of the gun.

Gigi It's not a toy.

Mimi It's not a game. Killing.

Gigi You wouldn't – you couldn't.

Mimi moves away from the window, raging round the room. Gigi stays by the window, checking.

Mimi Do you still not understand? I want . . . I want . . . I want . . . and nothing stops it. Nothing is ever big enough. I want to be heard. I want to scream and shout. I want to kill everybody in sight. I want to set the world on fire. Why am I being punished when I've done nothing bad? Why shouldn't the crime fit the punishment? Why shouldn't I do something that would give meaning to my life? Tell me!

Gigi But killing a child wouldn't give it meaning. A child is innocent. People would think you really were mad.

Mimi Am I?

Gigi No!

Mimi Am I?

Gigi No.

Mimi I'm giving you another chance. Am I mad?

Gigi No! You're in pain. But you're not mad.

Mimi Thank you.

Mimi lets herself be held.

Gigi (*relieved*) Besides, it's only a word.

Mimi Why do I feel you're tying me up, so I lose the thread?

Gigi Because if I agreed, if I said – yes, you're mad – it would be like giving you permission to let go. I have to keep you this side of reason. I often kill people in my head. Thinking is not the same as doing.

Mimi Thinking is driving me mad.

Gigi (*soothing*) Don't think any more. Leave things to me. Be like you used to be. Let Gigi wrap you up warm and prop you up with a pillow. You could take a nap and wake up when it's all done.

As Gigi wins back the ascendancy, she helps Mimi lie down, then goes back to the window, still checking.

Mimi (*very low*) I want it to stop.

Gigi Soon it will stop. We'll go away from here and we'll begin again. We'll be different this time.

Mimi If we don't know what made us go wrong, how can we be different? Gigi?

Gigi (*checked*) All we can do is try –

Mimi That's a lie! You think you know what went wrong. You think if you could just shed me, you'd be free. I'm your burden. I'm not just your sister. You said it yourself: I'm your history. If I died, you'd be glad. You could pretend I never existed. You could start again scratching yourself from scratch.

Gigi No. It's not true. Believe me. If you must read me, read me right. Sometimes at break of day before you wake, there is a blissful silence. No prattle. An absence of strife. Me, hardly there at all. I press my head into the pillow to feel my own life throbbing. I get up to fill the kettle: my own thirst makes me. Mine. The air clasps me like a cold embrace. A drop of water in the eye of the sink winks at me. I am all and only me. I eat a crust quietly to keep you asleep. But –

Mimi What?

Gigi It's hardly a life at all on my own. My mind is miniscule. You're my flesh and blood. I need you just as much as you need me. We belong to each other.

Appeased, Mimi reaches her arms around Gigi. They hold each other, comforting.
Suddenly in the street outside a vehicle comes to a halt. Car doors slam. Gigi checks the window.

Mimi What is it?

Gigi (*calm*) A van.

Mimi Stopping?

Gigi (*reassuring*) That's all right. It's all part of the plan.

Mimi Today?

Gigi Yes, I told you. Today is the day.

Mimi checks the window.

Mimi Three men.

There is a loud knocking at the house door.

Gigi (*prompt*) I'll go. (*Realising that she is still holding the gun, she stops herself.*) I can't –

The knocking continues. Mimi takes the gun.

Mimi I can. Do you believe me?

Gigi I don't want to believe you. I have to go down –

The knocking stops.

Mimi No! Listen!

Gigi Gone?

Mimi checks the window again.

Mimi One at the gate. One in the street. The other is still at the door.

Gigi I've got to go down.

Mimi Those men down there. (*taking aim*) Our fate.

Gigi Don't.

Mimi (*aiming*) Do you believe me now?

Gigi No.

Mimi You've got to believe me!

Gigi I believe you want to do it.

Mimi Talk-talk!

Gigi But I don't believe you will do it –

The knocking begins again. Mimi positions herself by the window so that she cannot be seen.

Mimi You want me to prove it!

Gigi No!

Mimi You do it then!

Gigi (*shrinking*) No!

Mimi (*giving the gun*) Kill those men –

Gigi No!

Mimi And we say something – loud and clear. Bloodsuckers sucking our blood!

Gigi No! (*pleading*) Nobody would hear. It would do no good.

Mimi Do it for Mimi.

Gigi No!

Mimi It's my say.

Gigi (*wild*) Why?

Mimi Because when you've got nothing, when you are nothing, you can't just lie down and die; or lie down and lick their boots; or sit up and beg for scraps and drool and play the fool and let them off the hook: you've got to fight back and if killing is the only way, you have to do it, because that's how you get back what you've lost. You become something again.

Gigi A thing!

Mimi A voice! You had your say. Now it's my turn.

Gigi (*pleading*) There must be a better way.

Mimi Too late!

Gigi No! Wait! Let's procrastinate. Let's think. Let's negotiate.

The knocking starts again very loud.

Mimi Actions speak louder than words. Let's do it together. Now, Gigi, now!

Together they hold the gun, taking aim, and then firing six times. Blackout.

There is a brief silence, then the same radio music as before and a faint grey light grows at the window. Mimi and Gigi are putting on their coats.

Gigi Ready?

Mimi Is it really today?

Gigi Today is always the day.

Mimi It's not too late?

Gigi It's never too late.

Mimi Let's begin then.

Gigi It's already begun.

Mimi (*helpful*) We could just keep smiling. We might even have fun.

Gigi It's true. Let's look on the bright side. One day – at twilight, say, a worn-out piano tinkling just out of key –

Mimi (*amending*) – off stage –

Gigi – when we're waiting quietly for the final curtain, we might be overjoyed by the sudden sight of a spider swinging on a sightless thread. On the other hand, we might just be walking along, minding our own business, nose down, rooting in the trash, and suddenly like a flash of inspiration, the sky might be irradiated; and the world might explode and we'd slip out of our skins and end up as shadows printed on the scorched earth. It's true. Given this situation, anything is possible.

Mimi We could just keep trying to get it right.

Gigi Let's play it that way.

They give a last look round, then go, leaving everything. The radio continues to play hesitant piano music. The light gradually fades to darkness.